MW00812574

Instant Pot Duo Crisp
Air Fryer Lid Cookbook 1000

Enjoy Simple Yet Nutritious Luscious Instant Pot Pressure Cooker and Air Fryer Recipes on A Budget for Any Smart People

By Judy Amanda

Contents

Chapter 6: Soups, Stews, and Broths

Chapter 7: Rice, Multi-grain, and Porridges..110

Chapter 8: Beans, Chilis, and Eggs 125

INTRODUCTION

The Instant Pot® that air fries.

In recent years, the instant pot has garnered numerous fans and for a positive reason.it replaces your slow cooker because its pressure cooker functions significantly shortens cooking time. Imagine making braised short ribs in it for less than 1 hour. Amazing right? Even better, you can set time and leave the food cooking unattended as you would on the stopover.

This Instant Pot Duo Crisp Air fryer Lid is a brilliant option if you want to add broiling, dehydrating, and air frying capabilities to your instant pot. Whether you are cooking for a large family, small family, or commercial purposes, this appliance is perfect for you.

Additionally, this game-changing accessory is easy to use. You cook directly in the instant pot and the inner pot but swap the regular lid with this Air fryer lid. You can even stow the lid in the cabinet when not in use. I would highly recommend this kitchen appliance to all Instant pots fans out there.

CHAPTER 1: Instant Pot Duo Crisp Air Fryer Lid 101

What is Instant Pot Duo Crisp with Air Fryer Lid?

This is a stand-alone lid that perfectly sits on your instant pot housing letting you broil, dehydrate, and air fry food. The Instant Pot Duo Crisp with air fryer lid turns your instant pot into a powerful air fryer. This kitchen appliance guarantees a golden finish and a crispy crunch to your food every single time.

The Instant Pot Duo Crisp with Air Fryer Lid is conveniently unattached to the cooker base. This makes it easy to maneuver and clean. The lid comes with a display screen that's clear to read and buttons for your various cooking methods

Constructions of It

One kitchen appliance, two lids

This amazing Instant Pot Duo Crisp Air Fryer Lid is a single gadget that comes with two lids. You simply swap the lids depending on the method of cooking you want to use.

Control panel

The control panel has several buttons and a bright dual display that helps control the Instant Pot Duo Crisp Air Fryer Lid when cooking. The display also won't turn on when the lid isn't fitted correctly

Multilevel fryer basket

This basket fits a surprising amount of food. For example, it can hold up to 16 chicken wings all at once which is sufficient unless you are cooking large batches of food.

Broiling tray

It's where you place your food when air frying or broiling to crisp them up

Protective pad

This is where you set the lid when it's hot. After the lid has cooled, you can flip it over to use as a storage cover.

Stay cool handle

The handle stays cool even when the Instant Pot Duo Crisp Air Fryer Lid is in use. It helps keep you safe from the heating element.

Accessories

Pressure Cooking lid

Multi-level air fryer basket

Air Fryer lid

Steam rack

Protective pad and storage cover

Broil/dehydrate tray

Know It's Amazing Functions

The decisive moment is here. So what does this Instant Pot Duo Crisp Air Fryer Lid do?

11 Smart Programs for ultimate one-pot cooking

Air-fry

This is a smart way to reduce the amount of oil used when frying food. It uses ht air to cook and crisp food better than in deep frying. It's ideal for crisping vegetables, fried chicken, and fried shrimps among others.

Bake

This Instant Pot Duo Crisp Air Fryer Lid serves as a mini oven and bakes everything that is bake-able ranging from desserts to casseroles. If using a cake pan, bake without covering it not unless the recipe calls for it. You should also bake at a temperature range of 180^0F to 380^0F

Roast

This function is excellent for all those pork, poultry, beef, and vegetable ideas in your mind. Roasting creates the best and perfectly crispy crust on meats and creates a delish golden brown exterior on vegetables

Dehydrate

This kitchen appliance can dehydrate jerky meats, fruit, vegetables the best. Using this Instant Pot Duo Crisp Air Fryer Lid to dehydrate food will make you want to give away your convection oven.

Broil

The broil function has the best direct to heating and creates the best-browned creme brulee, casseroles among others. The secret is to put your food in the fryer basket and set the temperature at 180F to 380F for 1 minute to 1 hour.

Reheating

While the instant pot has the keep warm function this Instant Pot Duo Crisp Air Fryer Lid has the reheating function. Reheating is perfect for crusted and crisped food. When reheating food place them in a safe-oven dish, fryer basket or broiling tray

The Work Principle

Below is a guide of how Instant Pot Duo Crisp Air Fryer Lid works.
1. If the instant pot was in use, unplug it from the power sauce and release all pressure. Remove the regular lid.

2. Place the Air fryer lid on the instant pot inner cooking pot and plug it in. the lid should perfectly fit inside the housing.
3. Select the cooking program of choice and customize the temperature and time using the [+] and [-] buttons. Press the start button to cook.
4. A "Turn Food" message appears when the food is halfway cooked. When you lift the lid cooking cycle pauses. Remember to place the lid on its protective pad. You may choose to ignore the message, especially when broiling food.
5. When the cooking time elapses, the Instant Pot Duo Crisp Air Fryer Lid displays "End". You can lift the lid and place the lid on the protective pad. Enjoy your food.

Tips for Usage

Attach the control panel

If the control panel is incorrectly connected, the Instant Pot Duo Crisp Air Fryer Lid will turn off. It's advisable to press the control panel until you hear a click.

Add oil

You should always add oil to the fryer before turning it on to avoid damage. You should preferably use the same type of oil as different types of oil can react with each other when heated.

When to change the oil

You should never allow the oil to be dirty in the first place. Always change the oil after ten uses or as soon as it tends to be dark, Smokey, or smelly. Moreover, if you use your Instant Pot Duo Crisp Air Fryer Lid to fry donuts and sandwiches you should consider renewing the oil more often.

Do not kill two birds with one stone

Never plug the instant pot and Air fryer lid at the same time. Doing so may destroy the lid, the base, or both. Connect one at a time

Clean the device well

Grease and oil may accumulate or spatter around the heating element during cooking. After each cook, a cooling cycle ensures to clean the Instant Pot Duo

Crisp Air Fryer Lid. this prevents smoke and fire which may cause personal injury.

Common FAQs

Ultimate one-pot meals.

What can I cook in my instant pot Air fryer lid?

The air fryer lid transforms your Instant pot into a two-in-one appliance giving you a wide range of foods the gadget can cook ranging from crispy chicken wings to vegetable chips at a press of a button.

Can I use aluminum foil in the Instant Pot Duo Crisp Air Fryer Lid?

Yes, you can use aluminum foil but it all depends on the food you are cooking. With most solid foods, you can just wrap them and throw them in the air fryer.

Must you put oil in the Instant Pot Duo Crisp Air Fryer Lid?

No, an air fryer cooks food by circulating air in the appliance with or without oil.

Can I use a glass bowl in the Instant Pot Duo Crisp Air Fryer Lid?

Yes, but you must use an oven-safe bowl in the air fryer whether it's ceramic, glass, silicon or metal

Can I bake in the Instant Pot Duo Crisp Air Fryer Lid?

Yes, you can bak in the Instant Pot Duo Crisp Air Fryer Lid. In fact, its super easy since you don have to preheat it like in the oven.

Chapter 2: Brunches

Baked Eggs

This is an easy breakfast recipe that is perfected with the Instant Pot Duo Crisp Air Fryer Lid. Try it now to understand the reason for the fuss. Prep time and cooking time: 30 minutes | Serves: 4

Ingredients To Use:

- 4 medium eggs
- 1 Tbsp. of olive oil
- 1 pound of torn baby spinach
- 4 Tbsp. of milk
- 7 ounces of chopped ham
- Salt and black pepper, as desired
- Cooking spray

Step-by-Step Directions to Cook It:

1. Heat the oil in a device compatible with the Instant Pot Duo Crisp Air Fryer Lid, then add the baby spinach and cook until tender.
2. Coat 4 ramekins with the cooking spray and fill it up with the ham and cooked baby spinach.
3. Add an egg to each ramekin, 1 Tbsp. of milk, and season with salt and pepper.
4. Transfer the ramekins to an oven-safe baking dish and place it in the Instant Pot cooker base.
5. Position the broil/dehydration tray, and cover with the Instant Pot Duo Crisp Air Fryer Lid.
6. Select the Bake Smart Program and adjust the time and temperature to 20 minutes and 350°F, respectively. Select *Start* to begin baking.
7. Serve for Breakfast.

Nutritional value per serving:

Calories: 321kcal, Fat: 6g, Carbs: 15g, Protein: 12g

Breakfast Souffle

A very light dish perfect for mornings. It is stress-free and can be prepared within 20 minutes.
Prep time and cooking time: 18 minutes | Serves: 4

Ingredients To Use:

- 1 medium onion, diced
- 4 Tbsp. of heavy cream
- 4 medium eggs, whisked
- A pinch of red chili pepper, crushed
- 2 Tbsp. of chopped chives
- 2 Tbsp. of chopped parsley + 1 tsp. to garnish
- Salt and black pepper, as desired

1. Mix the eggs, salt, black pepper, red chili pepper, onion, parsley, heavy cream, and chives in a medium bowl. Whish thoroughly.
2. Transfer the mixture to 4 soufflé dishes and arrange in the Instant Pot cooker base.
3. Fit the Instant Pot Duo Crisp Air Fryer Lid and select the Bake Smart Program. Adjust the time to 8 minutes and the temperature to 350°F—select *Start* to begin.
4. Remove, garnish with parsley, and serve immediately.

Nutritional value per serving:

Calories: 300kcal, Fat: 7g, Carbs: 15g, Protein: 6g

Egg Muffins

Muffins are easy to prepare and always ready to save the day. Try this recipe out now with the Instant Pot Duo Crisp Air Fryer Lid to understand the real meaning of scrumptious.
Prep time and cooking time: 25 minutes | Serves: 4

Ingredients To Use:

- 1 medium egg
- 2 Tbsp. of olive oil
- 3 Tbsp. of milk
- 3.5 ounces of white flour
- 1 Tbsp. of baking powder
- 1/2 cup of diced baby spinach
- 1 cup of yellow onion
- 1 cup of diced red and green pepper
- 2 ounces of grated parmesan
- A splash of Worcestershire sauce

Step-by-Step Directions to Cook It:

1. Mix the egg, flour, baking powder, baby spinach, bell pepper, oil, milk, Worcestershire sauce, and parmesan. Whisk thoroughly and serve into 4 muffin cups.
2. Transfer the cup to the air fryer and cover with the Instant Pot Duo Crisp Air Fryer Lid.
3. Select the Bake Smart Program and adjust the time to 15 minutes and the temperature to 392°F
4. Serve immediately.

Nutritional value per serving:

Calories: 251kcal, Fat: 6g, Carbs: 9g, Protein: 3g

Cinnamon Toast

Eat your toast crunchy and tasty with this cinnamon recipe.
Prep time and cooking time: 15 minutes | Serves: 6

Ingredients To Use:

- 1 stick of soft butter
- 12 bread slices

- 1/2 cup of sugar
- 1-1/2 tsp. vanilla extract
- 1-1/2 tsp. cinnamon powder

1. Mix the butter, sugar, cinnamon, and vanilla in a small bowl. Whisk thoroughly.
2. Spread the egg mixture on the bread slices and arrange them in the air fryer. Cover with the Instant Pot Duo Crisp Air Fryer Lid and select the Bake Smart Program. Set the timer to 5 minutes and the temperature 400°F
3. Serve the bread.

Nutritional value per serving:

Calories: 221kcal, Fat: 4g, Carbs: 12g, Protein: 8g

Egg Casserole

Taste the difference with this egg casserole recipe prepared with the Instant Pot Duo Crisp Air Fryer Lid. Prep time and cooking time: 35 minutes | Serves: 6

Ingredients To Use:

- 1 pound of ground turkey
- 1 Tbsp. of olive oil
- 1/2 tsp. of chili powder
- 12 medium eggs
- 1 sweet potato, cubed
- 1 cup of baby spinach
- Salt and black pepper, as desired

- 2 tomatoes, chopped for garnish

Step-by-Step Directions to Cook It:

1. Mix the eggs, salt, black pepper, sweet potato, turkey, chili powder, and spinach. Mix well.
2. Preheat the air fryer to 350°F, add the oil, then pour in the egg mix.
3. Spread the egg mix in the inner pot and cover with the Instant Pot Duo Crisp Air Fryer Lid.
4. Select the Bake Smart Program and adjust the time to 25 minutes and the temperature to 350°F
5. Scrape the egg mix out of the air fryer and serve warm.

Nutritional value per serving:

Calories: 300kcal, Fat: 5g, Carbs: 13g Protein: 6g

Sausage, Eggs and Cheese Mix

This recipe is a perfect blend of sausages, eggs, and cheese. The egg holds the sausage together, and the cheese adds creaminess to the meal. Prep time and cooking time: 30 minutes | Serves: 4

Ingredients To Use:

- 10 ounces of sausages, cooked and crumbled
- 1 cup of shredded cheddar

cheese
- 1 cup of shredded mozzarella cheese
- 8 medium eggs, whisked
- 1 cup of milk
- Salt and black pepper, as desired
- Cooking spray

Step-by-Step Directions to Cook It:

1. Mix the sausages, mozzarella, cheddar, eggs, salt, black pepper, and milk in a small bowl.
2. Preheat the Instant pot air fryer to 380°F and add the eggs and sausage mixture. Cover with the Instant Pot Duo Crisp Air Fryer Lid, Select the Bake Smart Program and adjust the time to 20 minutes.
3. Serve into plates.

Nutritional value per serving:

Calories: 320kcal, Fat: 6g, Carbs: 12g, Protein: 5g

Breakfast Egg Bowls

For mornings when you just want an easy recipe that can be prepared in a few minutes; this meal on the Instant Pot Duo Crisp Air Fryer Lid has got you covered.
Prep time and cooking time: 30 minutes | Serves: 4

Ingredients To Use:

- 4 dinner rolls, tops cut off and insides scooped out

- 4 medium eggs
- 4 Tbsp. of heavy cream
- 4 Tbsp. of grated parmesan
- 4 Tbsp. mixed chives and parsley
- Salt and black pepper, as desired

Step-by-Step Directions to Cook It:

1. Arrange the dinner rolls on a flat surface, add an egg to each roll, then spice with the mixed herbs and heavy cream—season with salt and black pepper.
2. Add the parmesan to the rolls and transfer them to the inner pot of the Instant Pot Air Fryer.
3. Position the dehydration tray, cover with the Instant Pot Duo Crisp Air Fryer Lid, and select the Bake Smart Program. Set the timer to 20 minutes and the temperature to 350°F. Click on Start to begin cooking.
4. Put each bread roll on a plate and serve.

Nutritional value per serving:

Calories: 238kcal, Fat: 4g, Carbs: 14g, Protein: 7g

Biscuits Casserole

Every bite comes with a unique combination of biscuit, sausages, and seasoning. The meal is healthy and highly delicious.
Prep time and cooking time: 25 minutes | Serves: 8

- 12 ounces of quartered biscuits
- 3 Tbsp. flour
- 1/2 pound of sausage, chopped
- A pinch of salt and black pepper
- 2-1/2 cup of milk
- Cooking spray

Step-by-Step Directions to Cook It:

1. Grease the inner pot of the air fryer with the cooking spray and preheat it to 350°F
2. Arrange the biscuits at the bottom of the pot, then layer it with the chopped sausage.
3. Mix the flour, salt, black pepper, and milk in a bowl, then transfer it to the inner pot. Cover with the dehydration tray and the Instant Pot Duo Crisp Air Fryer Lid.
4. Select the Bake Smart Program and adjust the time to 15 minutes.
5. Serve immediately.

Nutritional value per serving:

Calories: 321kcal, Fat: 4g, Carbs: 12g, Protein: 5g

Creamy Hash Browns

Do you want to start your mornings like royalty? Then try this recipe out with the Instant Pot Duo Crisp Air Fryer Lid, and you won't be disappointed.

Prep time and cooking time: 30 minutes | Serves: 6

Ingredients To Use:

- 2 pounds of hash browns
- 8 bacon slices, chopped
- 1 cup of whole milk
- 9 ounces of cream cheese
- 1 yellow onion, sliced
- 6 green onions, chopped
- 1 cup of shredded cheddar cheese
- 6 medium eggs
- Salt and black pepper, as desired
- Cooking spray

Step-by-Step Directions to Cook It:

1. Grease the inner pot of the air fryer with the cooking spray and preheat it to 350°F
2. Mix the eggs, milk, cheddar, cream cheese, onion, bacon, salt, and black pepper in a bowl. Whisk well.
3. Pour the hash browns and egg mix into the inner pot of the Instant Pot Air Fryer and cover with the Instant Pot Duo Crisp Air Fryer Lid.
4. Select the Bake Smart Program and adjust the time to 20 minutes. Click Start to begin cooking.
5. Divide into equal portions and serve.

Calories: 261kcal, Fat: 6g, Carbs: 8g, Protein: 12g

Asparagus Frittata

This is a lovely way to incorporate vegetables into your breakfast. With the Instant Pot Duo Crisp Air Fryer Lid, you can eat healthily and deliciously.
Prep time and cooking time: 15 minutes| Serves: 2

Ingredients To Use:

- 4 medium eggs, whisked
- 2 Tbsp. parmesan, grated
- 4 Tbsp. milk
- Salt and black pepper, as desired
- 10 asparagus tips, steamed
- Cooking spray

Step-by-Step Directions to Cook It:

1. Grease the inner pot of the Instant Pot air fryer with the cooking spray and preheat it to 400°F
2. Mix the eggs, milk, parmesan, salt, and black pepper in a bowl. Whisk thoroughly and add the asparagus.
3. Transfer the asparagus egg mixture to the inner pot and cover with the Instant Pot Duo Crisp Air Fryer Lid. Select the Bake Smart Program and cook for 5 minutes

4. Divide the frittata into equal portions and serve warm.

Nutritional value per serving:

Calories: 312kcal, Fat: 5 g, Carbs: 14g, Protein: 2g

Air-fried Scotch Eggs

The perfect breakfast or snack, especially when served with the chutney dipping sauce. You'll gonna love it!
Prep Time and cooking time: 20 minutes | Serves: 6

Ingredients To Use:

- 1 egg, lightly beaten
- 1 lb. bulk sausage, uncooked
- 5 hard-boiled eggs
- 1 tbsp. mustard or hot sauce
- Oil spray, for coating
- 1 cup almond flour or coconut flour

Step-by-Step Directions to cook it:

1. Peel the hard-boiled eggs and set aside.
2. Meanwhile, divide the sausage into 6 equal parts and flatten to form a 4-inch wide patty. Lay the boiled eggs in the center and wrap the patty around it. Repeat the process until you have used up all the eggs and sausage patties.
3. Dip each sausage-wrapped patty in the beaten egg and then into

almond flour for coating. Spray evenly all sides with oil.

4. Place wrapped patties in the air fryer, making sure they aren't overcrowded. You may use the second layer of the air fryer basket to accommodate all patties. Attach the instant pot duo crisp Air Fryer Lid and air fry at 400 degrees F for 12-16 minutes, turning halfway through cooking.
5. Once done, cut in halves and serve with mustard on top. You may also serve it with hot sauce.

Nutritional value per serving:

Calories: 407 kcal, Fat: 29.44 g, Carbs: 10.65 g, Protein: 24.91 g

Simple & Easy Mac and Cheese

A very quick and easy fix to a tasty side-dish. You'll gonna make this Simple Mac and Cheese in no time. Prep time and cooking time: 45 minutes | Serves: 6

Ingredients To Use:

- 2-1/2 cups macaroni
- 2-2/3 cups sharp cheddar or pepper jack, shredded
- 1 cup bread crumbs
- 2 cups chicken stock
- 1-1/4 cups heavy cream
- 1/3 cup Parmesan cheese, shredded
- 8 tbsps. butter, melted and divided
- 1/4 tsp. garlic powder
- Salt and pepper to taste

Step-by-Step Directions to cook it:

1. Place the metal inner pot in your instant pot and add the chicken broth.
2. Also add the heavy cream, 4 tablespoons of butter and macaroni.
3. Pressure cook on HIGH for about 20 minutes or until al dente.
4. Combine the bread crumbs with the remaining butter in a mixing bowl.
5. Quick-release the pressure and stir in 2 cups of sharp cheddar (or pepper jack), salt, pepper and garlic powder.
6. Top with the remaining ⅔ cup of sharp cheddar (or pepper jack), 1/3 cup of Parmesan cheese, and breadcrumb mixture.
7. Air fry at 400 degrees F for about 5 minutes or until browned.
8. Transfer into serving plates and enjoy!

Nutritional value per serving:

Calories: 680 kcal, Fat: 56 g, Carbs: 22 g, Protein: 22 g

Pepperoni Pasta

An irresistible golden, cheesy top. These Pepperoni Pasta is hearty and

filling. Good for dinner.
Prep time and cooking time: 30
minutes | Serves: 8

Ingredients To Use:

- 16 oz. rigatoni pasta
- 1 lb. Italian sausage
- 6 oz. pepperoni, sliced
- 1 (28 oz.) can diced Italian
  tomatoes, with juice
- 1 (28 oz.) can tomato puree
- 8 oz. Mozzarella cheese,
  shredded
- 2 cups chicken stock
- 1 cup red wine
- 1 medium onion, chopped
- 2 tbsps. garlic, minced
- 1/2 tsp. oregano
- 1/2 tsp. basil
- 1/4 tsp. red pepper, crushed
- 1/4 tsp. ground black pepper
- 1/2 tsp. salt

Step-by-Step Directions to
cook it:

1. Set the instant pot to SAUTE
   then cook the onions, sausage
   and garlic until browned.
2. Stir in the spices, salt, pepper,
   the chicken stock, red wine, and
   half of the pepperoni. Make sure
   that everything is well combined.
3. Add the tomato puree and
   tomatoes and stir lightly.
4. Pour in the pasta, gently
   pressing down to ensure that it's
   covered with liquid. Don't stir so
   that the pasta will be kept at the

bottom of the pot.
5. Pressure cook on HIGH for about
   6 minutes or until al dente.
6. Quick-release and remove the lid.
7. Add in 1/3 of the cheese then stir
   well. Add the remaining cheese
   on top and layer the rest of the
   pepperoni on top of the cheese.
8. Attach the air fryer lid to the
   instant pot and air-fry at 400
   degrees F for 5 minutes.
9. Once cooked, remove the lid and
   serve the pepperoni pasta.

Nutritional value per serving:

Calories: 581 kcal, Fat: 33 g, Carbs: 42
g, Protein: 29 g

Big Bite Sandwich

Italian sausages and hot dog buns
are the key to this Big Bite Sandwich.
It's easy to throw this together in no
time at all.
Prep time and cooking time: 18
minutes | Serves: 6

Ingredients To Use:

- 6 Italian sausages
- 1-1/2 cups of water
- 6 hot dog buns

Step-by-Step Directions to
cook it:

1. Pour about 1-1/2 cups of water
   into the inner steel pot. Set the
   trivet and the basket inside the
   pot, coating the bottom part of
   the basket with nonstick spray.

2. Place the sausage links inside, making sure that they're not overlapping each other.
3. Close the pot with pressure cooker lid and steam valve. Adjust the setting to HIGH and cook for 5 minutes.
4. Quick-release and remove the lid then spritz the links with cooking spray.
5. Cover the lid and air fry at 400 degrees F for 8 minutes. Flip halfway through the cooking process so that both sides get browned.
6. Remove from the pot and serve in buns.

Nutritional value per serving:
Calories: 408 kcal, Fat: 24.7 g, Carbs: 26.5 g, Protein: 20 g

Cheesy Air Fryer Spaghetti

Mixed with spaghetti noodles, parmesan cheese grated, mozzarella cheese and you will have this delicious Cheesy Air Fryer Spaghetti. Prep time and cooking time: 24 minutes | Serves: 6

Ingredients To Use:
- 1 lb. ground beef
- 1 (24 oz.) jar spaghetti sauce
- 8 oz. spaghetti noodles, broken into thirds
- 1-1/2 cups Mozzarella cheese, grated and divided
- 1/2 cup Parmesan cheese grated
- 2 cups beef broth
- 1 onion, diced
- 1 green onion, diced (optional)
- 2 tbsps. olive oil
- 1/4 tsp. salt

Step-by-Step Directions to cook it:
1. Set the instant pot to SAUTE then drizzle the bottom of the steel pot with olive oil.
2. Sauté the onions and ground beef then season with salt. Continue to cook until the ground beef is no longer pink.
3. Evenly spread the cooked meat to cover the bottom of the pot entirely.
4. Pour the spaghetti sauce then add the broth into the jar. Put the lid back on and shake the jar to mix the meat and broth with the remaining sauce. Pour the broth into the pot but do not stir.
5. Sprinkle the broken spaghetti noodles on top of the liquid.
6. Using a spoon spatula, gently submerge the noodles into the sauce but do not stir.
7. Place the pressure cooker lid and close the steam valve.
8. Pressure cook on HIGH for 9 minutes.
9. Quick-release and remove the lid.
10. Stir in one cup of mozzarella cheese until it melts.
11. Sprinkle the remaining half cup

of the mozzarella cheese plus the parmesan on top of the spaghetti. Top with the diced green onions then closes the pot with air fryer lid.

12. Air fry at 400degrees F for 5 minutes, until the cheese melts and gets golden brown on top.
13. Serve and enjoy.

Nutritional value per serving:

Calories: 338 kcal, Fat: 14 g, Carbs: 37 g, Protein: 16 g

Healthy Breakfast Bake

You can prepare this Healthy Breakfast Bake ahead of time because this easy to bake is infinitely adaptable!
Prep time and cooking time: 31 minutes | Serves: 2

Ingredients To Use:

- 1 slice whole grain bread, torn into pieces
- 4 eggs
- 1-1/2 cups baby spinach
- 1/2 cup bell pepper, diced
- 2 tbsps. 1% low-fat milk
- 1 tsp. hot sauce
- 1/2 tsp. Kosher salt
- 1/4 cup + 2 tbsps. shredded cheddar cheese, divided

Step-by-Step Directions to cook it:

1. Preheat your air fryer to 250 degrees F. Spritz a 6-inch soufflé dish with nonstick spray and set aside.
2. In a medium bowl, add the beaten eggs, hot sauce, milk and salt.
3. Gently fold in the spinach, 1/4 cup cheddar, bread pieces and bell peppers.
4. Pour the egg mixture into the prepared soufflé dish and place the dish into the air fryer basket.
5. Set up the trivet to the inner pot of the cooker and place the basket on top.
6. Cook at 250 degrees F for 20 minutes. Sprinkle the top with the remaining cheese and cook for another 5 minutes or until the eggs are set and the edges are golden brown.
7. Remove from the air fryer basket and set aside for about 10 minutes before serving.

Nutritional value per serving:

Calories: 173 kcal, Fat: 9 g, Carbs: 14 g, Protein: 9 g

Perfect Bacon & Croissant Breakfast

Full of protein and high in energy, these perfect bacon and croissant is a "make it in a hurry" filling breakfast.
Prep time and cooking time: 15 minutes | Serves: 2

Ingredients To Use:

- 4 pieces thick-cut bacon
- 2 croissants, sliced
- 2 eggs
- 1 tbsp. butter
- For the bacon barbecue sauce:
- 1/2 cup ketchup
- 2 tbsps. apple cider vinegar
- 1 tbsp. brown sugar
- 1 tbsp. molasses
- 1/2 tbsp. Worcestershire sauce
- 1/4 tsp. onion powder
- 1/4 tsp. mustard powder
- 1/4 tsp. liquid smoke

Step-by-Step Directions to cook it:

1. Preheat your air fryer to 390 degrees F.
2. Meanwhile, incorporate all the barbecue sauce ingredients in a small saucepan. Place the pan over medium heat and bring it to a simmer until the sauce thickens slightly.
3. Place the bacon cuts flat on a tray and brush them with barbecue sauce on one side.
4. Transfer to the air fryer basket with the brushed-side up. Cook for about 4-5 minutes then flip the bacon. Brush the other side with bacon sauce and cook for another 5 minutes (or until your desired doneness is achieved).
5. In a medium-size frying pan, melt the butter and fry the eggs

according to your preference.
6. Once done, place the eggs at the bottom of each croissant. Top them with two bacon slices each and close with the croissant on top.
7. Serve with your favorite breakfast beverage.

Nutritional value per serving:

Calories: 643 kcal, Fat: 39 g, Carbs: 57 g, Protein: 16 g

Air-fried French Toast Sticks

Buttered this French Toast Sticks and reheat it in air fryer to make the most delicious breakfast. So quick and easy to make.
Prep time and cooking time: 17 minutes | Serves: 2

Ingredients To Use:

- 4 pcs. sandwich bread
- 2 tbsps. butter, softened
- 2 eggs, gently beaten
- 1 pinch ground cloves
- 1 pinch cinnamon
- 1 pinch nutmeg
- 1 pinch salt
- 1 tsp. maple syrup, for garnish

Step-by-Step Directions to cook it:

1. Preheat your air fryer to 350 degrees F.
2. Meanwhile, add the beaten eggs,

cinnamon, nutmeg, ground cloves and salt in a bowl.

3. Butter both sides of the bread slices and cut them into strips.
4. Dredge each bread strip in the egg mixture, letting the excess liquid mixture drip completely. Arrange them in your air fryer basket; work in two batches if necessary.
5. Place the air fryer trivet in the inner steel pot of your cooker and place the basket on top of it.
6. Air fry for 2 minutes and generously spritz the sticks with cooking spray. Flip the sticks and spray the other side as well.
7. Air fry for another 4 minutes, keeping an eye on them just to make sure they don't burn. They're done when the sticks are golden brown.
8. Remove from the air fryer and transfer to a serving plate. Drizzle with maple syrup before serving. If desired, you can also sprinkle them with icing sugar and top with whip cream.

Nutritional value per serving:

Calories: 163 kcal, Fat: 15 g, Carbs: 2 g, Protein: 5 g

Ranchero Brunch Crunch Wraps

Easy and quick to make. These ranchero brunch crunch wraps is spicy brunchwrap version of the original favorite.

Prep time and cooking time: 20 minutes | Serves: 2

Ingredients To Use:

- 2 servings tofu scramble (or vegan egg)
- 2 large flour tortillas
- 2 small corn tortillas
- 1/3 cup pinto beans, cooked
- 1/2 cup classic ranchero sauce
- 1/2 avocado, peeled and sliced
- 2 fresh jalapeños, stemmed and sliced

Step-by-Step Directions to cook it:

1. Assemble the large tortillas on a work surface. Arrange the crunch wraps by stacking the following ingredients in order: tofu or egg scramble, jalapeños, ranchero sauce, corn tortillas, avocado, and pinto beans. You can add more ranchero sauce if desired.
2. Fold the large flour tortilla around the fillings until sealed completely.
3. Place one crunch wrap in the air fryer basket and set the basket on top of the trivet.
4. Air-fry each crunch wrap at 350 degrees F (or 180°C) for 6 minutes. Remove from the basket and transfer to a plate.

5. Repeat step 3 and 4 for the other crunch wrap.

Nutritional value per serving:

Calories: 290 kcal, Fat: 14 g, Carbs: 26 g, Protein: 15 g

Crunchy Breakfast Nuggets

This is easy and a quick kids meal. Just put olive oil in air fryer and fry it. Monitor them to make sure they are not over cooked.

Prep time and cooking time: 50 minutes | Serves: 4

Ingredients To Use:

- 1 lb. boneless, skinless chicken breasts
- 2/3 cup whole wheat panko bread crumbs
- 1/3 cup Parmesan cheese, freshly grated
- 1/4 cup whole wheat flour
- 1 large egg
- 2 tsps. dried parsley flakes
- Olive oil spray
- 1/4 tsp. salt or to taste
- 1/4 tsp. black pepper

For dipping sauce (optional):

- 1 tbsp. marinara
- 1 tbsp. ranch dressing
- 1 tbsp. barbecue sauce

Step-by-Step Directions to cook it:

1. Preheat your air fryer 400 degrees F for about 8-10 minutes. Meanwhile, slice the chicken breasts into 1-inch cubes.
2. Prepare three shallow bowls; mix the flour, salt, and pepper in the first bowl. Lightly beat the egg in the second and combine the parmesan, panko, and parsley flakes in the third.
3. Working one piece at a time, dredge the chicken in the flour mixture and press lightly to adhere. Next, dip it into the egg, removing the excess egg as needed. Finally, coat with the Panko mixture, pressing lightly to help evenly coat the chicken.
4. Arrange the nuggets in the air fryer basket in a single layer. Liberally spritz them with cooking spray to help them get crispy and golden brown.
5. Air-fry each batch for about 7 minutes or until the internal temperature reaches 165 degrees F (or 74°C). Monitor them to make sure that they're not overcooked.
6. Serve with your favorite dip and your favorite side dish.

Nutritional value per serving:

Calories: 402 kcal, Fat: 8 g, Carbs: 34 g, Protein: 46 g

Chapter 3: Red Meat Recipes

Oriental Air Fried Lamb

Here, the lamb is air fried for 8 minutes to improve the flavor and texture before adding to the stock.
Prep time and cooking time: 52 minutes | Serves: 8

Ingredients To Use:

- 2-1/2 pounds of chopped lamb shoulder
- 3 Tbsp. honey
- 3 ounces of chopped almonds, peeled
- 8 ounces of veggie stock
- 9 ounces of pitted plumps
- 2 yellow onions, chopped
- 1 tsp. cinnamon powder
- 2 garlic cloves, minced
- Salt and black pepper, as desired
- 1 tsp. ginger powder
- 1 tsp. cumin powder
- 1 tsp. turmeric powder
- 3 Tbsp. olive oil

Step-by-Step Directions to Cook It:

1. Preheat the Instant Pot to 350°F
2. Mix the cinnamon, ginger, turmeric, cumin, olive oil, garlic, and lamb. Ensure the lamb is adequately coated.
3. Transfer the seasoned lamb to the air fryer basket and cover it with Instant Pot Air Fryer Lid.
4. Select the Air Fry Smart Program and adjust the time to 8 minutes. You will be notified when it's time to *"Turn Food."*
5. Transfer the lamb to an oven-safe baking dish, add the onions, veggie stock, plums, and honey. Stir.
6. Cover with the Instant Pot Duo Crisp Air Fryer Lid and cook for 35 minutes at 350°F
7. Divide into equal portions and serve.

Nutritional value per serving:

Calories: 332kcal, Fat: 23g, Carbs: 30g, Protein: 20g

Short Ribs and Special Sauce

The combination of spices and sauce in this recipe infuses flavor into the lamb. Each bite of the lamb will take you on an adventure to discover the cause of the rich flavor.
Prep time and cooking time: 46 minutes | Serves: 4

Ingredients To Use:

- 2 green onions, chopped
- 1 tsp. vegetable oil
- 3 garlic cloves, grated

- 3 ginger slices
- 1/2 cup of soy sauce
- 4 pounds of short ribs
- 1/2 cup of water
- 1/4 cup of pear juice
- 1/4 cup of rice wine
- 2 tsp. sesame oil

Step-by-Step Directions to Cook It:

1. Using the Instant Pot cooker base, select Sauté and heat the oil, then add the green onions, garlic, and ginger. Fry for a full minute, then press Cancel.
2. Add the wine, soy sauce, sesame oil, water, pear juice, and ribs to the inner pot.
3. Add the broil/dehydration tray, cover with the Instant Pot Duo Crisp Air Fryer Lid, and select the Broil Smart Program. Set the timer for 30 minutes and the temperature for 350°F
4. Divide ribs into 4 portions and serve immediately.

Nutritional value per serving:

Calories: 321kcal, Fat: 12g, Carbs: 20g, Protein: 14g

Roasted Pork Belly and Apple Sauce

The lamb is coated with apple and lemon before roasting to allow for maximum absorption of flavor. The lemon gives the lamb a sharp,

pleasant after taste.
Prep time and cooking time: 50 minutes | Serves: 6

Ingredients To Use:

- 2 Tbsp. sugar
- 1 quart of water
- 1 Tbsp. lemon juice
- 17 ounces of apples, cut into wedges
- A drizzle of olive oil
- 2 pounds of scored pork belly
- Salt and black pepper, as desired

Step-by-Step Directions to Cook It:

1. To a food processor, add the apples, sugar, and lemon juice. Pulse well to obtain a smooth mixture.
2. Coat the pork with the smooth mixture and set the rest aside.
3. Transfer the seasoned pork to the air fryer basket, position the broil, dehydration tray, and cover with the Instant Pot Duo Crisp Air Fryer Lid.
4. Select the Roast Smart Program and set the timer for 40 minutes at 400°F.
5. Remove the lamb after roasting and set aside.
6. Pour the reserved apple mix into the inner pot of the air fryer and cover with the Instant Pot Duo Crisp Air Fryer Lid. Select the Broil Smart Program and set the

timer for 15 minutes at 300°F

7. Carve the lamb and serve with the sauce drizzled over the top.

Nutritional value per serving:

Calories: 456kcal, Fat: 34g, Carbs: 10g, Protein: 25g

Lemon Glazed Lamb

Glazing the lamb with lemon infuses it with a rich flavor that can be tasted when eating the lamb. This recipe will leave you eager for more.

Prep time and cooking time: 40 minutes | Serves: 4

Ingredients To Use:

- 2 lamb shanks
- Salt and black pepper, as desired
- 2 garlic cloves, minced
- 4 Tbsp. olive oil
- Juice from 1/2 lemon
- Zest from 1/2 lemon
- 1/2 tsp. oregano, dried

Step-by-Step Directions to Cook It:

1. Rub the lamb with garlic and season with salt and black pepper. Transfer to the air fryer basket of the instant Pot Air fryer.
2. Secure the Instant Pot Duo Crisp Air Fryer Lid, select the Roast Smart Program, and set the timer for 40 minutes at 400°F.
3. While the lamb is roasting, mix the rest of the ingredients to make the lemon dressing. Add

salt and black pepper to improve the taste.

4. Every 10 minutes, coat the lamb with the lemon dressing using a brush. Exercise caution while removing the Instant Pot Duo Crisp Air Fryer Lid.
5. Shred the lamb and serve.

Nutritional value per serving:

Calories: 260kcal, Fat: 7g, Carbs: 15g, Protein: 12g

Creamy Ham and Cauliflower

The 1 hour used for cooking in this recipe is to allow the ham to fully absorb the essence of the chicken stock and cauliflower juice. The result is fantastic.

Prep time and cooking time: 1 hour 10 minutes | Serves: 6

Ingredients To Use:

- 8 ounces of grated cheddar cheese
- 14 ounces of chicken stock
- 4 cup of cubed ham
- 1/2 tsp. garlic powder
- 4 garlic cloves, grated
- 1/2 tsp. onion powder
- Salt and black pepper, as desired
- 1/4 cup of heavy cream
- 16 ounces of cauliflower florets

Step-by-Step Directions to Cook It:

1. To a spring form pan that fits

your Instant Pot Air fryer, add the ham, chicken stock, cauliflower, and cheddar cheese.
2. Add the onion powder, garlic powder, garlic, salt, heavy cream, and black pepper. Stir and transfer to the Air Fryer.
3. Add the broil/dehydration tray, cover with the Instant Pot Duo Crisp Air Fryer Lid, and select the Broil Smart program.
4. Set the timer for 1 hour at 300°F.
5. Press Start to begin cooking.
6. Divide into equal portions and serve.

Nutritional value per serving:

Calories: 320kcal, Fat: 20g, Carbs: 16g, Protein: 23g

Instant Air Fried Sausage and Mushrooms

The sausages and the mushroom slices are air-fried until they are crunchy and tasty. The fact that only a tsp of oil is used for frying is a marvel that is best performed with the Instant Pot Duo Crisp Air Fryer Lid.
Prep time and cooking time: 50 minutes | Serves: 6

Ingredients To Use:

- 3 red bell peppers, sliced
- 1 Tbsp. brown sugar
- 2 pounds of sliced pork sausage
- 2 pounds of sliced Portobello mushrooms
- 2 sweet onions, chopped
- Salt and black pepper, as desired
- 1 tsp. olive oil

Step-by-Step Directions to Cook It:

1. In an oven-safe baking dish, mix the sausages with salt, black pepper, oil, mushrooms, bell pepper, sugar, and onions. Toss until the sausages and mushrooms are well-coated.
2. Transfer the coated mixture to the Instant Pot Air fryer and cover with the Instant Pot Duo Crisp Air Fryer Lid.
3. Select the Air Fry Smart Program and set the timer for 40 minutes at 300°F.
4. Serve immediately.

Nutritional value per serving:

Calories: 130kcal, Fat: 12g, Carbs: 13g, Protein: 18g

Sausage and Kale Soup

Healthy and delicious. It can only get better when cooking with the Instant Pot Duo Crisp Air Fryer Lid
Prep time and cooking time: 30 minutes | Serves: 4

Ingredients To Use:

- 1 cup of yellow onion, chopped
- 1 cup of water
- 1-1/2 pound of sliced Italian pork sausage

- 1/2 cup of chopped red bell pepper
- 5 pounds of chopped kale
- 1 tsp. garlic, grated
- Salt and black pepper, as desired
- 1/4 cup of chopped red hot chili pepper

Step-by-Step Directions to Cook It:

1. In a springform pan that fits the Instant Pot Air Fryer, mix the sausage slices, salt, pepper, onion, bell pepper, garlic, kale, chili pepper, and water.
2. Transfer the pan to the air fryer, cover with the Instant Pot Duo Crisp Air Fryer Lid, and select the Broil Smart Program.
3. Adjust the time to 20 minutes and the temperature to 300°F
4. Divide into equal portions and serve.

Nutritional value per serving:

Calories: 150kcal, Fat: 4g, Carbs: 12g, Protein: 14g

Sirloin Steaks and Pico De Gallo

Experience a burst of flavor with this spice-rich recipe. The steaks are first seasoned with the first set of spices, then combined with the second set of spices after cooking.
Prep time and cooking time:20 minutes | Serves: 4

Ingredients To Use:

- 2 Tbsp. chili powder
- 1 tsp. garlic powder
- 4 medium sirloin steaks
- 1 tsp. cumin, ground
- 1 tsp. onion powder
- 1/2 Tbsp. sweet paprika
- Salt and black pepper, as desired
- Lemon wedges for garnish.

Pico de Gallo Ingredients:

- 1 small red onion, chopped
- 1/4 cup of chopped cilantro
- 2 tomatoes, chopped
- 2 garlic cloves, grated
- 1 small green bell pepper, chopped
- 1 jalapeno, chopped
- 2 Tbsp. lime juice
- 1/4 tsp. of ground cumin

Step-by-Step Directions to Cook It:

1. Mix the chili powder, black pepper, salt, garlic powder, onion powder, 1 tsp. cumin, and paprika in a small bowl. This will serve as the rub.
2. Season the steaks with the rub and transfer them to the air fryer basket. Add the broil/dehydration tray and cover with the Instant Pot Duo Crisp Air Fryer Lid.
3. Select the Roast Smart Program and set the timer for 10 minutes at 360°F.

4. In a separate bowl, mix the Pico de Gallo Ingredients until they are well combined.
5. Serve the steaks with the Pico de Gallo mix after cooking. Garnish with lemon wedges

Nutritional value per serving:

Calories: 200kcal, Fat: 12g, Carbs: 15g, Protein: 18g

Coffee Flavored Steaks

You don't have to rely on only espressos for your dose of coffee; you can also get it from your meals with this coffee glazed rib eye steaks. Prep time and cooking time: 25 minutes | Serves: 4

Ingredients To Use:

- 1-1/2 Tbsp. of ground coffee
- A pinch of cayenne pepper
- 4 rib-eye steaks
- 1/4 tsp. of ground coriander
- 1/2 Tbsp. sweet paprika
- 2 tsp. garlic powder
- 2 Tbsp. chili powder
- 2 tsp. onion powder
- 1/4 tsp. ginger, ground
- Black pepper, as desired

Step-by-Step Directions to Cook It:

1. Mix the ground coffee, paprika, garlic, chili powder, coriander, onion powder, cayenne, garlic powder, and black pepper in a small bowl. This will serve as the rub.
2. Season the steaks with the rub, transfer it to the air fryer basket, and cover it with the Instant Pot Duo Crisp Air Fryer Lid.
3. Select the Roast Smart Program and set the timer for 15 minutes at 360°F.
4. Divide the steaks into equal portions and serve with salad

Nutritional value per serving:

Calories: 160kcal, Fat: 10g, Carbs: 14g, Protein: 12g

Beef Kabobs

The skewers are first coated with an excellent combination of spices and then roasted until they are tasty and delicious.
Prep time and cooking time: 20 minutes| Serves: 4

Ingredients To Use:

- 2 red bell peppers, chopped
- 1/4 cup of salsa
- 2 pounds of chopped sirloin steak
- 1 red onion, chopped
- Juice from 1 lime
- 2 Tbsp. chili powder
- 1 zucchini, sliced
- 2 Tbsp. of hot sauce
- 1/2 Tbsp. of ground cumin
- 1/4 cup of olive oil
- Salt and black pepper, as desired

1. Mix the salsa, hot sauce, lime juice, chili powder, salt, cumin, and black pepper in a small bowl.
2. Arrange the meat, zucchini, onions, and bell pepper on a skewer. Repeat the process until the ingredients are exhausted.
3. Coat the kabobs with the rub prepared earlier, transfer to the air fryer, and cover with the Instant Pot Duo Crisp Air Fryer Lid.
4. Select the Roast Smart Program and set the timer for 10 minutes at 370°F.
5. Flip the skewers after 5 minutes.
6. Serve immediately with salad.

Nutritional value per serving:

Calories: 170kcal, Fat: 5g, Carbs: 13g, Protein: 16g

Instant pot with Air fryer Lid Pot Roast

This is the best instant pot roast you will ever have. It's cooked in the instant pot then air fried for a crazy crispy and delicious ending.
Prep Time and Cooking Time: 1 hour 20 minutes| Serves: 6

Ingredients to use:

- 2-1/2 lb. chuck roast
- 1-1/2 tbsp. garlic powder
- Salt and pepper

- 1-1/2 lb. baby potatoes
- 1 lb. baby carrots
- Fresh herbs

Step-by-step Directions to Cook It:

1. Add water to the instant pot and place a trivet. Place the roast on the trivet and cook on high pressure for 1 hour.
2. Quick-release pressure and add potatoes and carrots. Cook for more minutes oh high pressure.
3. Let the instant pot release pressure naturally for 5 minutes then quickly release the rest of the pressure.
4. Remove the instant pot lid and replace it with the air fryer lid.
5. Select air fry and set the temperature to 450°F and the time for 5 minutes.
6. Serve and enjoy.

Nutritional value per serving:

Calories: 54kcal, Carbs: 9g, Fat: -g, Protein: -g

Instant pot Air Fryer Lid Frozen Meatballs

These straight from the freezer meatballs are super easy to cook and are surprisingly the sweetest. The meatballs are perfect for a crowd-pleaser appetizer.
Prep Time and Cooking Time: 20 minutes| Serves: 3

Ingredients to use:

- 1 lb. frozen meatballs
- Oil spray
- BBQ sauce or tomato sauce

Step-by-step Directions to Cook It:

1. Place the meatballs in the air fryer basket in a single layer. Place the basket in the instant pot and seal the instant pot with an air fryer lid.
2. Select the air fry function and set the temperature to 380⁰F and the timer for 10 minutes.
3. Meanwhile, heat the BBQ sauce on a saucepan and serve with the meatballs. Enjoy.

Nutritional value per serving:

Calories: 398kcal, Carbs: -g Fat: 32g, Protein: 26g

Pork Belly Bites

If you are a fan of crispy pork, then this recipe is for you. The belly bites come out so good that you will want to make them over and over again. Prep Time and Cooking Time: 30 minutes| Serves: 4

Ingredients to use:

- 1 lb. pork belly
- 1 tbsp. Worcestershire sauce
- 1/2 tbsp. garlic powder
- Salt and pepper
- 1/4 cup BBQ sauce

Step-by-step Directions to Cook It:

1. Cut the pork belly into 3/4 inch cubes and place them in a bowl.
2. Season the pork cubes with sauce, garlic, salt, and pepper. Spread the pork in an air fryer basket in a single layer. Place the basket in the instant pot and seal the instant pot with an air fryer lid.
3. Select the air fry function and set the temperature to 400⁰F and the timer for 15 minutes.
4. Drizzle with more salt and pepper and serve warm with BBQ sauce if you like.

Nutritional value per serving:

Calories: 590kcal, Carbs: 1g Fat: 60g, Protein: 11g

Best Beef Taquitos

This beef taquitos serve scrumptious appetizers and can be doubled to serve a delicious and filling dinner. They require minimal preparation and will be loved by everyone Prep Time and Cooking Time: 60 minutes| Serves: 20

Ingredients to use:

- 2 lb. beef chuck
- 1 tbsp. garlic, minced
- 1 cup white onion, chopped
- 1 cup canned tomatoes, chopped
- Salt and pepper to taste

- 1 tbsp. lime juice
- 2 tbsp. orange juice
- 2 tbsp. olive oil
- 2 tbsp. chipotle
- 1 tbsp. smoked paprika
- 1 tbsp. garlic powder
- 1 tbsp. cumin, ground
- 1 tbsp. chili powder
- 4 cups beef broth
- 1/2 cup cilantro
- 2 cups mozzarella cheese and cheddar cheese, shredded
- 20 mini tortillas

Step-by-step Directions to Cook It:

1. Set the instant pot to sauté function and season the meat with salt, pepper, and paprika.
2. Place the meat in the instant pot and cook until well seared on all sides. Set aside
3. Add tomatoes and other spices in the instant pot and stir well to combine. Select cancel.
4. Place the meat on top of the spice mixture and add beef broth. The broth should cover half the meat.
5. Pressure cook on high for 35 minutes then quick-release pressure. Remove the meat from the instant pot and use forks to shred it.
6. Empty the inner pot of the instant pot then clean it and dry it well. Return the inner pot and

place the air fryer basket with a trivet in.
7. Mix the cooked meat, cilantro, and cheese in a mixing bowl then place the filling in each tortilla and roll it.
8. Place the taquitos in the trivet and seal the instant pot with the air fryer lid. Select broil and set time for 5 minutes.
9. Use tongs to remove the taquitos and enjoy them.

Nutritional value per serving:

Calories: 390kcal, Carbs: 46g Fat: 17g, Protein: 13g

Pork Chops

This is the ultimate way to cook pork chops. They are crazy simple to make and the end result is deliciously moist.
Prep Time and Cooking Time: 24 minutes| Serves: 1

Ingredients to use:

- 4 pork chops
- 1 egg
- 1/2 almonds, coarsely ground
- 1/2 cup parmesan cheese, grated

Step-by-step Directions to Cook It:

1. Beat egg in a mixing bowl, then mix almonds and cheese in a separate bowl.
2. Dip pork chops in the egg then coat them in the cheese mixture

until well covered.

3. Place the chops in an air fryer basket and place the basket in the instant pot. Seal the instant pot with the air fryer lid and set time for 14 minutes.
4. The chops should reach an internal temperature of 145^{0}F.
5. Remove the chops from the instant pot and let rest for 10 minutes before serving.

Calories: 502kcal, Carbs: 5g Fat: 31g, Protein: 49g

BBQ Ribs

These BBQ ribs are first pressure cooked that makes them fall off the born tender. They, therefore, can be eaten by everyone including the kids
Prep Time and Cooking Time: minutes| Serves: 2

Ingredients to use:

- 700g pork ribs
- BBQ sauce of your choice

Step-by-step Directions to Cook It:

1. Pour water in the instant pot and place the trivet in place. Place the ribs on the trivet.
2. Pressure cook the ribs for 15 minutes then release the pressure naturally.
3. Discard the water and clean the inner pot. Dry it and place back

the ribs. Smother them with BBQ sauce.

4. Seal the instant pot with an air fryer lid and set the temperature to 204^{0}F and timer for 5 minutes.
5. Serve and enjoy.

Calories: 280kcal, Carbs: 17g Fat: 15g, Protein: 20g

Countryside Ribs

This finger-licking deliciously tender countryside ribs are easy to make and so flavourful that you will not get enough of them.
Prep Time and Cooking Time: 1hour 30 minutes| Serves: 5

Ingredients to use:

- 1 tbsp. garlic powder
- 1 tbsp. onion powder
- 2 tbsp. soy sauce
- 1/2 cup apple cider vinegar
- 3/4 cup of cold water
- 4 lb. country-style ribs
- 1/2 tbsp. salt
- Black pepper
- 2 tbsp. brown sugar
- 1 cup BBQ sauce

Step-by-step Directions to Cook It:

1. Add garlic powder, onion powder, soy sauce, vinegar, and water in the instant pot. Mix until well combined.
2. Place the ribs in the marinade

and add salt, pepper, and sugar. Mix well and let marinate for 1 hour in the fridge.

3. Place the inner pot in the instant pot and pressure cook for 15 minutes at high pressure then naturally release the pressure.
4. Remove the cooking liquid and add 1 cup of water in the pot. Place the air fryer basket with a tray on the middle rack. Place the ribs in the tray and seal the instant pot with an air fryer lid.
5. Select the air fry function and set the temperature to 400°F and timer for 12 minutes.
6. Serve immediately with baked beans or salad

Nutritional value per serving:

Calories: 373kcal, Carbs: 11g Fat: 20g, Protein: 34g

Easy Instant pot with Air fryer lid Ribs

Brushed with sweet and Smokey barbecue sauce, these ribs are finger licking delish. They serve a perfect weeknight dinner that every member of your family will love.
Prep Time and Cooking Time: 40 minutes| Serves: 3

Ingredients to use:

- 1 rack baby back ribs
- Salt and pepper
- 1/4 cup BBQ sauce of choice
- A few drops of liquid smoke

Step-by-step Directions to Cook It:

1. Remove the membrane from the ribs and season them with salt and pepper.
2. Add 1 cup of water to the instant pot and place a trivet. Place the ribs on the trivet and close the lid. Pressure cook for 25 minutes on high pressure then naturally release the pressure.
3. Empty the inner pot then clean it and dry it well.
4. Place the air fryer basket in the inner pot then rub the ribs with sauce and liquid smoke. Place the ribs in the basket.
5. Seal the instant pot with the fryer lid and select the air fry function. Set temperature to 450°F and timer for 15 minutes.
6. Remove the ribs from the instant pot and serve.

Nutritional value per serving:

Calories: 348kcal, Carbs: 7g Fat: 23g, Protein: 27g

Instant Pot Duo Crisp Crisp Pork Ribs

These juicy, tender ribs with sauce caramelized on them are the best crowd-pleaser dish to serve during family gatherings or holiday celebrations.

Prep Time and Cooking Time: 1 hour 10 minutes| Serves: 4

Ingredients to use:

- 1 rack pork ribs
- Rib rub
- 1-1/2 cup beef broth
- 3 tbsp liquid smoke
- 1 cup BBQ sauce

Step-by-step Directions to Cook It:

1. Remove membrane from the ribs the cut the rack into two.
2. Rub the rack with rib rub on all sides.
3. Add beef broth to the instant pot then place the ribs in their fryer basket with the meat side down. Place the basket on a trivet.
4. Pressure cook the ribs on high pressure for 30 minutes then naturally release pressure for 15 minutes.
5. Remove the ribs from the instant pot and rub with liquid smoke and BBQ sauce then return them to the air fryer basket.
6. Select the air fry function and set the temperature to 400⁰F and timer for 20 minutes.
7. Serve and enjoy.

Nutritional value per serving:

Calories: 216kcal, Carbs: 35g Fat: 6g, Protein: 5g

T Bone steak

There is nothing amazing than this simple T Bone steak made from your Instant pot with air fryer lid. You can season it as much as you like to make it your favorite.

Prep Time and Cooking Time: 20 minutes| Serves: 2

Ingredients to use:

- T-bone steak, trimmed
- Salt
- Pepper
- Garlic

Step-by-step Directions to Cook It:

1. Put the steak in the instant pot Air fryer lid basket then put the basket in the instant pot.
2. Seal the instant pot with air fryer lid and select the air fry function. Set temperature to 400⁰F and the timer for 14 minutes.
3. When the steak is halfway cooked, season to your liking.
4. Let the steak sit for some minutes before serving. Enjoy.

Nutritional value per serving:

Calories: 54kcal, Carbs: 9g Fat: -g, Protein: -g

Instant Pot Duo Crisp BBQ Bacon Meatloaf

If looking for something interesting, simple, and quick to make to serve for busy weeknight dinners, look no further. This meatloaf is a solid choice for you.

Prep Time and Cooking Time: 35 minutes| Serves: 8

Ingredients to use:

- 1/2 cup milk
- 3 slices of bread
- 2lb ground beef
- 3/4 cup parmesan cheese, grated
- 1 tbsp. salt
- 1/4 tbsp. seasoned salt
- Black pepper, freshly ground
- 3 egg, beaten
- 2 tbsp. parsley, dried
- 8 slices of bacon
- 1/2 cup BBQ sauce, divided

Step-by-step Directions to Cook It:

1. In a mixing bowl, pour milk over bread and let it soak for a few minutes.
2. Add beef, cheese, salts, pepper, eggs, and parsley. Mix until well combined.
3. Fold an aluminum foil sheet into 16" by 7" sling.
4. Mold the meat mixture into a loaf at the center of the sling leaving a 4" of the foil on each side that will be used as handles.
5. Lay the bacon on the loaf tucking the ends underneath the loaf. Spread half of the BBQ sauce over the bacon.
6. Pour 2 cups of water in the instant pot and place a trivet. Lower the meatloaf onto the trivet and fold the sling ends so that they don't interfere with the lid.
7. Lock the lid and cook on high pressure for 20 minutes. Quick-release pressure and check the internal temperature of the meatloaf. It should be 155^{0}F otherwise cook for more minutes.
8. Use the sling to remove the meatloaf from the instant pot.
9. Discard the cooking liquid and wash and dry the inner pot. Return the trivet and lower the meatloaf onto it.
10. Spread the remaining BBQ sauce on the meatloaf and Lock the instant pot using the air fryer lid and select the broil function. Set temperature to 400^{0}F and time for 8 minutes.
11. Use the sling to remove the meatloaf from the instant pot and let rest for a few minutes before serving.

Nutritional value per serving:

Calories: 500kcal, Carbs: 16g Fat: 14g, Protein: 41g

Stuffed Peppers

These stuffed peppers are a colorful, flavorful and great easy dish to serve for dinner parties or for entertaining guests.

Prep Time and Cooking Time: 45 minutes| Serves: 8

Ingredients to use:

- 1 tbsp. olive oil
- 1 lb. ground beef
- Salt and ground black pepper
- 4 large cremini mushrooms, sliced
- 1 onion, minced
- 1 tbsp. soy sauce
- 8 bell peppers, tops, and cores removed. Dice the tops
- 1 tbsp. Italian seasoning
- 1 cup white rice, cooked
- 1 tbsp. tomato paste
- 6 garlic cloves, minced
- 1 tbsp. soy sauce
- 1/4 cup smoked cheddar cheese, shredded
- 1/4 cup mozzarella cheese, shredded
- 1 can tomatoes, diced
- Parsley for garnish, chopped

Step-by-step Directions to Cook It:

1. Press the sauté function on the instant pot and wait until it heats up. Add oil and ensure the bottom is well coated.
2. Season one side of beef with salt and pepper then place it in the instant pot seasoned side down. Add mushrooms to the side and let the beef brown.
3. Season the other side with salt and pepper then chop the beef and flip it. Cook until there is no cooking juice is left.
4. Break the beef into small chunks then mix with the mushrooms until well combined. Sauté for an additional 3 minutes.
5. Add onions and soy sauce in the instant pot. Sauté for 2 minutes. Add diced pepper tops and Italian seasoning. Sauté for 2 more minutes.
6. Add rice, tomato paste, and garlic. Sauté for 30 seconds. Break up the rice lumps ensuring the rice don't stick together. Remove the inner pot from heat.
7. Mix in the cheese and diced tomatoes into the stuffing. Fill the bell peppers with the stuffing while placing them on a trivet.
8. Clean the inner pot and dry it. Lower the trivet in the instant pot and seal with an air fryer lid.
9. Select air fry function then set the temperature to 400⁰F and the timer for 8 minutes
10. Garnish with parsley and serve.

Nutritional value per serving:

Calories: 285kcal, Carbs: 18g Fat: 17g, Protein: 16g

Instant Pot Duo Crisp Air Fryer Lid Spare Ribs

These ribs are finger-licking delicious. They are flavorful, super easy to make, and simply the best ribs to serve your family or friends
Prep Time and Cooking Time: 60 minutes| Serves: 3

Ingredients to use:

- 1 rack spare ribs
- 1 tbsp. garlic powder
- 1 tbsp. onion powder
- 2 tbsp. apple cider vinegar
- Salt and pepper
- 3 drops liquid smoke
- 1 cup cold water
- 1/2 cup BBQ

Step-by-step Directions to Cook It:

1. Remove flap at the end of each spare rib and separate the rib tips.
2. In a mixing bowl, mix garlic, onion, and vinegar until well mixed. Brush the ribs with the marinade.
3. Season the ribs with salt and pepper and let marinate in the fridge.
4. Add liquid smoke and water to the instant pot. Place the steam rack and lower the ribs on the rack.
5. Close the lid and cook on high pressure for 20 minutes. Release pressure naturally for 15 minutes then quickly release the rest. Empty the cooking liquid and wash the inner pot.
6. Place the air fryer basket with a dehydrating tray on the rack in the instant pot. Layer the ribs on the tray and seal the instant pot with air fryer lid.
7. Select the air fry function then set time to 400⁰F and timer for 15 minutes.
8. Chop the ribs ti serving sized and serve with your favorite BBQ sauce. Enjoy.

Nutritional value per serving:

Calories: 396kcal, Carbs: 8g Fat: 31g, Protein: 20g

Honey Garlic Ribs

These are sticky Chinese ribs made with few ingredients that are readily available in your pantry. They are so delicious that they will be your new weakness.
Prep Time and Cooking Time: 60 minutes| Serves: 4

Ingredients to use:

- 1 rack baby back ribs
- 6 garlic cloves, minced
- 2 tbsp. peanut oil
- 1/4 cup honey
- 3 tbsp. dark soy sauce
- Black pepper, ground

Marinade

- 1 tbsp. regular soy sauce
- 1/4 tbsp. fine salt
- 1/4 tbsp. sesame oil
- 1 tbsp. Shaoxing wine
- 1 tbsp. garlic powder

Step-by-step Directions to Cook It:

1. Mix the marinade ingredients in a Ziploc bag then add the baby back ribs. Let marinate for 2 hours.
2. Meanwhile, set the instant pot to sauté setting. When hot add garlic and sauté in peanut oil for 45 seconds
3. Add honey, soy sauce, and black pepper. Cook until the sauce has reduced and thickened.
4. Add 1 cup of water to the instant pot and place the trivet. Place the ribs on the trivet and close the lid.
5. Cook at high pressure for 16 minutes then naturally release pressure for 10 minutes.
6. Empty the inner pot and wash it. Place the air fryer basket with a dehydrating tray on the rack in the instant pot.
7. Layer the lids on the tray and close the instant pot using an air fryer lid. Select Broil function then set the temperature to 400⁰F and the timer for 15 minutes

8. Chop the ribs and brush them with honey before serving.

Nutritional value per serving:

Calories: 357kcal, Carbs: 15g Fat: 23g, Protein: 23g

Instant Pot Duo Crisp Air fryer Lid Lamb Jerky

Lamb jerky is so easy to make and the best brunch to serve. If you just purchased your Instant Pot Duo Crisp Air fryer lid, then this is a recipe you must try

Prep Time and Cooking Time: 3 hours 20 minutes| Serves: 1.5 lb jerky

Ingredients to use:

- 5 lb. lamb roast
- Hi Mountain Jerky Seasoning
- 5 tbsp. liquid smoke
- 1 tbsp. Dale Steak Seasoning

Step-by-step Directions to Cook It:

1. Slice the meat to 1/4 inch thick slices removing the silver skin.
2. Rub the jerky seasoning on the meat then place it in a sealable bag.
3. Add liquid smoke and Dale seasoning. Massage it until well covered. Let sit in the fridge for 24 hours.
4. Place the meat on a rack in the instant pot making sure you leave a space between each

piece.

5. Seal the instant pot with an air fryer lid and select dehydrate. Set temperature to 180°F and the timer for 3 hours. Flip the meat every hour.

Nutritional value per serving:

Calories: 219kcal, Carbs: 0g Fat: 17g, Protein: 89g

Stuffed Bell Peppers

Stuffed bell peppers makes the best easy dinner idea any night of the week. Mixed with sweet red, yellow and orange bell peppers.

Prep time and cooking time: 33 minutes | Serves: 6

Ingredients To Use:

- 6 bell peppers, cut the top and remove seeds
- 1/4 cup mozzarella cheese, shredded
- 1/4 cup cheddar cheese, shredded
- 1 tbsp. soy sauce
- 1 tsp. Italian seasoning
- 1 onion, minced
- 1 tbsp. garlic, minced
- 1 tbsp. tomato paste
- 14 oz. can tomatoes, diced
- 4 mushrooms, chopped
- 1 lb. ground beef
- 1 tbsp. olive oil
- 1 cup cooked rice
- Pepper
- Salt

Step-by-Step Directions to cook it:

1. Add oil into the instant pot and set the pot on saute mode.
2. Add meat and mushrooms into the pot and season with pepper and salt and saute for 5 minutes.
3. Add onion and soy sauce and saute for 2 minutes.
4. Add Italian seasoning and saute for 2 minutes.
5. Add cooked rice, garlic, and tomato paste and stir until well combined and cook for 1 minute.
6. Turn off the instant pot. Add can tomatoes and stir until well combined.
7. Remove meat mixture from instant pot and clean the instant pot.
8. Stuff meat mixture into the bell peppers.
9. Pour 1 cup of water into the instant pot then place the trivet in the pot.
10. Place stuff bell peppers on top of the trivet.
11. Seal the pot with pressure cooking lid and cook on high pressure for 5 minutes.
12. Once done, release pressure using the quick-release method. Open the lid.
13. Remove stuffed peppers from pot and clean the pot.
14. Place steam rack in the instant

pot then place stuffed peppers on top of the rack.

15. Mix together mozzarella and cheddar cheese and sprinkle on top of bell peppers.
16. Seal pot with air fryer lid and select air fry mode and set the temperature to 400 F and timer for 8 minutes.
17. Serve and enjoy.

Nutritional value per serving:

Calories: 365, Fat: 9.6 g, Carbs: 40.5 g, Protein: 29.4 g

Steak Tips

Mouthwatering skillet dish, quick and easy to make. Delicious Steak Bites mixed in a savory spicy garlic sauce.
Prep time and cooking time: 35 minutes | Serves: 3

Ingredients To Use:

- 1 lb. steak, cut into 3/4-inch cubes

For marinade:

- 1/8 tsp. cayenne pepper
- 1 tsp. Montreal steak seasoning
- 1/2 tsp. onion powder
- 1/2 tsp. garlic powder
- 1 tsp. olive oil
- Pepper
- Salt

Step-by-Step Directions to cook it:

1. In a bowl, add steak cubes and all marinade ingredients and toss well.
2. Spray instant pot multi-level air fryer basket with cooking spray.
3. Add marinated steak cubes into the air fryer basket and place basket in the pot.
4. Seal pot with air fryer lid and select air fry mode then set the temperature to 400 F and timer for 5 minutes.
5. Serve and enjoy.

Nutritional value per serving:

Calories 320 Fat 9.1 g Carbs 0.7 g Protein 54.7 g

Beef Kabobs

Skewered with potatoes, colorful veggies, peppers and onions. Beef Kabobs are the perfect summer idea for grilling season.
Prep time and cooking time: 20 minutes | Serves: 2

Ingredients To Use:

- 1/2 lb. beef chuck, cut into 1-inch pieces
- 1/4 onion, cut into 1-inch pieces
- 1 tbsp. soy sauce
- 2-1/2 tbsp. sour cream
- 1/2 bell pepper, cut into 1-inch pieces

Step-by-Step Directions to cook it:

1. In a mixing bowl, mix together meat, soy sauce, and sour cream. Cover and place in the refrigerator overnight.
2. Thread marinated meat, bell peppers, and onions on soaked wooden skewers.
3. Spray instant pot multi-level air fryer basket with cooking spray.
4. Place skewers into the air fryer basket and place basket into the instant pot.
5. Seal pot with air fryer lid and select air fry mode then set the temperature to 400 F and timer for 10 minutes. Turn skewers halfway through.
6. Serve and enjoy.

Nutritional value per serving:

Calories 262 Fat 10.3 g Carbs 4.8 g Protein 35.8 g

Simple Rib Eye Steak

Simple rib eye steak is tasty and delicious. Pan seared with the best garlic herb butter!
Prep time and cooking time: 24 minutes | Serves: 2

Ingredients To Use:

- 2 medium rib-eye steaks
- 1/2 tsp. garlic powder
- Pepper
- Salt

Step-by-Step Directions to cook it:

1. Season steaks with garlic powder, pepper, and salt.
2. Place the dehydrating tray in a multi-level air fryer basket and place basket in the instant pot.
3. Place steaks on dehydrating tray.
4. Seal pot with air fryer lid and select air fry mode then set the temperature to 400 F and timer for 14 minutes. Turn steaks halfway through.
5. Serve and enjoy.

Nutritional value per serving:

Calories 312 Fat 25 g Carbs 0.5 g Protein 20.1 g

Steak Tips with Potatoes

Served with crispy herbed potatoes, these steak tips with potatoes are so tender, easy and flavor packed dinner.
Prep time and cooking time: 30 minutes | Serves: 2

Ingredients To Use:

- 1/2 lb. steak, cut into 1/2-inch cubes
- 1/4 lb. potatoes, cut into 1/2-inch cubes
- 1/4 tsp. garlic powder
- 1/2 tsp. Worcestershire sauce
- 1 tbsp. butter, melted
- Pepper
- Salt

1. Cook potatoes into the boiling water for 5 minutes. Drain well and set aside.
2. In a mixing bowl, toss together steak cubes, potatoes, garlic powder, Worcestershire sauce, butter, pepper, and salt.
3. Spray instant pot multi-level air fryer basket with cooking spray.
4. Add steak potato mixture into the air fryer basket and place basket into the instant pot.
5. Seal pot with air fryer lid and select air fry mode then set the temperature to 400 F and timer for 20 minutes. mix halfway through.
6. Serve and enjoy.

Nutritional value per serving:

Calories 318 Fat 11.5 g Carbs 9.4 g Protein 42 g

Asian Beef Broccoli

These Asian beef broccoli is so tasty and delicious. Tender, juicy beef and broccoli smothered in a special glossy sauce.
Prep time and cooking time: 25 minutes | Serves: 3

Ingredients To Use:

- 1/2 lb. steak, cut into strips
- 1 tsp. garlic, minced
- 1 tsp. ginger, minced

- 2 tbsp. sesame oil
- 2 tbsp. soy sauce
- 1/3 cup oyster sauce
- 1 lb. broccoli florets

Step-by-Step Directions to cook it:

1. Add steak into the mixing bowl. Add remaining ingredients and mix well and set aside for 1 hour.
2. Spray instant pot multi-level air fryer basket with cooking spray.
3. Add marinated steak pieces and broccoli into the air fryer basket and place basket into the instant pot.
4. Seal pot with air fryer lid and select air fry mode then set the temperature to 350 F and timer for 15 minutes. mix halfway through.
5. Serve and enjoy.

Nutritional value per serving:

Calories 295 Fat 13.4 g Carbs 12.4 g Protein 32.4 g

Mushrooms & Steak Bites

Cooked in garlic butter sauce. These mushrooms and steak bites is so simple to make.
Prep time and cooking time: 30 minutes | Serves: 2

Ingredients To Use:

- 1/2 lb. steaks, cut into 1-inch cubes
- 1/4 tsp. garlic powder

- 1/2 tbsp. Worcestershire sauce
- 1 tbsp. butter, melted
- 4 oz. mushrooms, sliced
- Pepper
- Salt

1. In a mixing bowl, toss together steak cubes, mushrooms, garlic powder, Worcestershire sauce, butter, pepper, and salt.
2. Spray instant pot multi-level air fryer basket with cooking spray.
3. Add steak mushroom mixture into the air fryer basket and place basket into the instant pot.
4. Seal pot with air fryer lid and select air fry mode then set the temperature to 400 F and timer for 20 minutes. mix halfway through.
5. Serve and enjoy.

Nutritional value per serving:

Calories 294 Fat 11.6 g Carbs 2.9 g Protein 42.9 g

Delicious Fajitas

These delicious fajitas are so easy to prepare and easy to cook. Top them off with sour cream or add some chili powder, cayenne, or paprika.
Prep time and cooking time: 18 minutes | Serves: 2

Ingredients To Use:

- 1/2 lb. beef, sliced

- 1/2 tsp. garlic powder
- 1/2 tsp. paprika
- 3/4 tsp. cumin
- 1/4 tbsp. chili powder
- 1 1/2 tbsp. olive oil
- 1/4 onion, sliced
- 1 bell pepper, sliced
- Pepper
- Salt

Step-by-Step Directions to cook it:

1. Add meat and remaining ingredients into the mixing bowl and toss well.
2. Spray instant pot multi-level air fryer basket with cooking spray.
3. Add meat mixture into the air fryer basket and place basket into the instant pot.
4. Seal pot with air fryer lid and select air fry mode then set the temperature to 390 F and timer for 8 minutes. mix halfway through.
5. Serve and enjoy.

Nutritional value per serving:

Calories 335 Fat 18.2 g Carbs 7.5 g Protein 35.6 g

Juicy Steak

The key to a juicy steak is cook it FROZEN. Easy to prepare and easy to cook. Best serve in dinner.
Prep time and cooking time: 30 minutes | Serves: 2

- 2 steaks, 3/4-inch thick
- 1/2 tsp. garlic powder
- 1/4 tsp. onion powder
- 1 tsp. olive oil
- Pepper
- Salt

Step-by-Step Directions to cook it:

1. Coat steak with olive oil and season with garlic powder, onion powder, pepper, and salt.
2. Place the dehydrating tray in a multi-level air fryer basket and place basket in the instant pot.
3. Place steaks on dehydrating tray.
4. Seal pot with air fryer lid and select air fry mode then set the temperature to 400 F and timer for 20 minutes. Turn steaks halfway through.
5. Serve and enjoy.

Nutritional value per serving:

Calories 543 Fat 15.4 g Carbs 0.8 g Protein 94.4 g

Juicy & Crispy Meatballs

It'll bring Italy straight to you in this juicy and crispy meatballs. Juicy texture and slightly salty taste.
Prep time and cooking time: 25 minutes | Serves: 4

Ingredients To Use:

- 1 lb. ground beef

- 1/2 tsp. Italian seasoning
- 2 garlic cloves, minced
- 1/4 cup milk
- 1/2 cup parmesan cheese, grated
- 1/2 cup breadcrumbs
- Pepper
- Salt

Step-by-Step Directions to cook it:

1. Add all ingredients into the mixing bowl and mix until well combined.
2. Place the dehydrating tray in a multi-level air fryer basket and place basket in the instant pot.
3. Make small meatballs and place them on a dehydrating tray.
4. Seal pot with air fryer lid and select air fry mode then set the temperature to 375 F and timer for 15 minutes. Turn meatballs halfway through.
5. Serve and enjoy.

Nutritional value per serving:

Calories 312 Fat 10.7 g Carbs 11.5 g Protein 40.4 g

Simple Burger Patties

You can choose any toppings you want in your Simple Burger Patties! Super fast and easy to cooked.
Prep time and cooking time: 22 minutes | Serves: 4

Ingredients To Use:

- 1 lb. ground beef

- 1/2 tsp. garlic powder
- 1/2 tsp. onion powder
- 1/4 tsp. red pepper flakes
- Pepper
- Salt

Step-by-Step Directions to cook it:

1. Add all ingredients into the mixing bowl and mix until well combined.
2. Place the dehydrating tray in a multi-level air fryer basket and place basket in the instant pot.
3. Make four patties from meat mixture and place on dehydrating tray.
4. Seal pot with air fryer lid and select air fry mode then set the temperature to 350 F and timer for 12 minutes. Turn patties halfway through.
5. Serve and enjoy.

Nutritional value per serving:

Calories 213 Fat 7.1 g Carbs 0.6 g Protein 34.5 g

Chapter 4: Poultry Recipes

Honey Duck Breasts

The first coating is for the overall taste of the duck breast, while the second coating is to ensure that the deliciousness sticks to the duck's skin. Every bite of this meal tastes amazing.

Prep time and cooking time: 32 minutes | Serves: 2

Ingredients To Use:

- 1 smoked duck breast, halved
- 1 tsp. of honey
- 1 tsp. of tomato paste
- 1 Tbsp. of mustard
- 1/2 tsp. apple vinegar

Step-by-Step Directions to Cook It:

1. Mix the tomato paste, honey, mustard, vinegar, and duck breasts in a bowl.
2. Transfer the coated duck to the air fryer, cover with the Instant Pot Duo Crisp Air Fryer Lid, and select the Air Fry Smart Program. Set the timer for 15 minutes at 370°F.
3. Remove the duck and recoat with the honey mix, then return to the air fryer for another round of cooking. Set the timer for 6 minutes.
4. Divide into equal portions and serve.

Nutritional value per serving:

Calories: 274kcal, Fat: 11g, Carbs: 22g, Protein: 13g

Chicken and Parsley Sauce

You are missing a lot if you've never tried coating chicken with red wine before roasting or grilling. The taste is out of this world. Try it now with the Instant Pot Duo Crisp Air Fryer Lid, and you won't regret it.

Prep time and cooking time: 55 minutes | Serves: 6

Ingredients To Use:

- 1 cup of chopped parsley
- 12 chicken drumsticks
- 1 tsp. of dried oregano
- 1/2 cup of olive oil
- 4 garlic cloves
- 2 carrots, chopped
- A pinch of salt
- 1/4 cup of red wine
- A drizzle of maple syrup

Step-by-Step Directions to Cook It:

1. To a food processor, add the wine, oregano, parsley, salt, oil, garlic, and maple syrup. Pulse

until a smooth mixture is obtained.

2. Add the chicken to the red wine mix and keep in the refrigerator for 30 minutes.
3. Remove chicken from the mixture and transfer to the air fryer basket. Reserve the red wine mix.
4. Cover the Instant Pot cooker base with the Instant Pot Duo Crisp Air Fryer Lid and select the Roast Smart Program and set the timer for 25 minutes at 380°F.
5. Turn the food when the appliance brings up the notification.
6. Serve with reserved parsley sauce. Garnish with chopped carrots

Nutritional value per serving:

Calories: 354kcal, Fat: 10g, Carbs: 22g, Protein: 17g

Chicken and Green Onions Sauce

The green onions add a unique aroma and taste to the chicken. Try this recipe out to discover the real meaning of delicious.
Prep time and cooking time: 26 minutes | Serves: 4

Ingredients To Use:

- 10 green onions, coarsely chopped
- 1 Tbsp. lime juice
- inch piece ginger root, chopped
- 1/4 cup of chopped cilantro
- 4 garlic cloves, grated
- 1 tsp. butter, melted
- 2 Tbsp. fish sauce
- 3 Tbsp. soy sauce
- 1 tsp. Chinese five-spice
- 1 cup of coconut milk
- 10 chicken breasts
- Salt and black pepper, as desired

Step-by-Step Directions to Cook It:

1. Add the green onion, ginger, soy sauce, garlic, fish sauce, salt, five-spice, black pepper, coconut milk, and butter to a food processor and pulse until smooth.
2. Coat the chicken with the coconut milk mix, transfer to an oven-safe baking dish, and place it in the Instant Pot air fryer. Cover with the Instant Pot Duo Crisp Air Fryer Lid and select the Broil Smart Program and set the timer for 16 minutes at 370°F.
3. Shake the fryer after 10 minutes of cooking.
4. Serve hot.

Nutritional value per serving:

Calories: 321kcal, Fat: 12g, Carbs: 22g, Protein: 20g

Baked Greek Chicken

Baking is another method that allows you to cook chicken without consuming a lot of oil. Here, the trace amount of olive oil is used to make the ingredients stick to the skin of the chicken breasts.

Prep time and cooking time: 25 minutes | Serves: 4

Ingredients To Use:

- 2 Tbsp. olive oil
- Juice from 1 lemon
- 1 tsp. of dried oregano
- 3 garlic cloves, grated
- 1 pound of chicken breasts
- Salt and black pepper, as desired
- 1/2 pound ofof trimmed asparagus
- 1 zucchini, roughly chopped
- 1 lemon sliced

Step-by-Step Directions to Cook It:

1. In an oven-safe baking dish, mix the breasts, oil, oregano, lemon juice, asparagus, garlic, oregano, salt, lemon slice, zucchini, and black pepper. Stir until chicken is well-coated.
2. Transfer the baking dish to the Instant Pot air fryer and cover with the Instant Pot Duo Crisp Air Fryer Lid.
3. Select the Bake Smart Program and set the timer for 15 minutes at 380°F.
4. Divide into plates and serve.

Nutritional value per serving:

Calories: 300kcal, Fat: 8g, Carbs: 20g, Protein: 18g

Cider-Glazed Chicken

The chicken is briefly infused with flavor during the initial sautéing and then allowed to marinate for a few minutes before cooking with the rest of the ingredients.

Prep time and cooking time: 24 minutes | Serves: 4

Ingredients To Use:

- 1 sweet potato, cubed
- 1 Tbsp. mustard
- 2 apples, cored and sliced
- 1 Tbsp. butter
- 1 Tbsp. olive oil
- 1 Tbsp. rosemary, chopped
- 6 chicken thighs, bone-in and skin-on
- 2/3 cup of apple cider
- Salt and black pepper, as desired
- 1 Tbsp. butter
- 2 Tbsp. honey

Step-by-Step Directions to Cook It:

1. Using the Instant Pot cooker base, select Sauté, and heat the oil. Add the honey, cider, butter, and mustard. Stir and bring to a simmer. Add the chicken for a

brief moment to coat, then remove from heat and set aside.

2. Mix the apples, rosemary, oil, salt, and black pepper in a medium bowl. Add to the reserved chicken.
3. Transfer the coated chicken and mixture to the inner pot of the air fryer and cover with the Instant Pot Duo Crisp Air Fryer Lid.
4. Select the Broil Smart Program and adjust the time to 14 minutes and the temperature to 390°F
5. Divide into plates and serve.

Calories: 241kcal, Fat: 7g, Carbs: 28g, Protein: 22g

Turkey, Peas, and Mushroom Casserole

The turkey and chicken stock adds pizzazz to this delicious mushroom casserole.
Prep time and cooking time: 30 minutes | Serves: 4

Ingredients To Use:

- 1 cup of bread cubes
- 2 pounds of turkey breasts, skinned and deboned
- 1 yellow onion, sliced
- 1/2 cup of peas
- 1 celery stalk, sliced
- 1 cup of chicken stock
- 1 cup of cream mushrooms soup
- Salt and black pepper, as desired

Step-by-Step Directions to Cook It:

1. In a springform pan, mix the turkey, salt, onion, pepper, celery, stock, and peas.
2. Transfer the pan to the Instant Pot cooker base, add the broil/dehydration tray, and cover with the Instant Pot Duo Crisp Air Fryer Lid.
3. Set the timer for 15 minutes at 360°F.
4. Open the Instant Pot Duo Crisp Air Fryer Lid, add the cream of mushroom soup and bread cubes, and cover the air fryer again. Cook at the same temperature for 5 more minutes.
5. Divide into equal portions and serve immediately.

Nutritional value per serving:

Calories: 271kcal, Fat: 9g, Carbs: 16g, Protein: 7g

Chicken Tenders and Flavored Sauce

Do you like your chicken deliciously air fried and yummy? Then this recipe is perfect for you.
Prep time and cooking time: 30 minutes | Serves: 6

Ingredients To Use:

- 1 tsp. chili powder
- 2 tsp. garlic powder

- 1 tsp. onion powder
- 1 tsp. sweet paprika
- Salt and black pepper, as desired
- 2 Tbsp. butter
- 2 Tbsp. olive oil
- 2 pounds of chicken tenders
- 2 Tbsp. cornstarch
- 1/2 cup of chicken stock
- 2 cups of heavy cream
- 2 Tbsp. water
- 2 Tbsp. parsley, chopped

Step-by-Step Directions to Cook It:

1. Mix the garlic powder, onion powder, salt, black pepper, chili, and paprika in a medium bowl. This will serve as the rub.
2. Coat the chicken tenders with the rub, drizzle with oil, and place in the Instant Pot cooker base.
3. Cover with the Instant Pot Duo Crisp Air Fryer Lid and select the Air Fry Smart Program. Set the timer for 10 minutes at 360°F.
4. After air frying, set the chicken aside.
5. Set the empty cooker base to Sauté mode and melt the butter. Stir in the chicken stock, cornstarch, cream, parsley, and water. Cover with the Instant Pot Duo Crisp Air Fryer Lid and set to the Broil Smart Program for 10 minutes at 360°F.
6. Serve the chicken on plates and drizzle with the sauce.

Nutritional value per serving:

Calories: 351kcal, Fat: 12g, Carbs: 20g, Protein: 17g

Chicken and Radish Mix

Experience finger-licking goodness with this fantastic chicken and vegetable meal.
Prep time and cooking time: 40 minutes | Serves: 4

Ingredients To Use:

- 4 chicken things, bone-in
- Salt and black pepper, as desired
- 1 Tbsp. olive oil
- 1 cup of chicken stock
- 6 radishes, halved
- 1 tsp. sugar
- 3 carrots, cut into thin rounds
- 2 Tbsp. chives, chopped

Step-by-Step Directions to Cook It:

1. Set the empty cooker base to Sauté mode and heat the stock. Stir carrots, radishes, and sugar. Cover with the Instant Pot Duo Crisp Air Fryer Lid and set to the Broil Smart Program for 20 minutes at 360°F. Set the sauce aside.
2. Season the chicken with salt and black pepper, then rub with oil.
3. Transfer the chicken to air fryer basket, cover with the Instant Pot Duo Crisp Air Fryer Lid, and set to the Air Fry Smart Program.

4. Set the timer for 4 minutes at 350°F—select Start to begin.
5. When the chicken is done, add the radish sauce to the Instant Pot cooker base and cook for another 4 minutes.
6. Divide into equal portions and serve immediately.

Nutritional value per serving:

Calories: 237kcal, Fat: 10g, Carbs: 19g, Protein: 29g

Chicken Breast with Passion Fruit Sauce

The passion fruit adds a tropical flavor to the chicken. The fragrance also combines well with the aroma of the chicken.
Prep time and cooking time: 20 minutes | Serves: 4

Ingredients To Use:

- 4 chicken breasts
- Salt and black pepper, as desired
- 4 passion fruits, halved, deseeded and pulp reserved
- 1 Tbsp. whiskey
- 2-star anises
- 2 ounces maple syrup
- 1 bunch chives, chopped

Step-by-Step Directions to Cook It:

1. Set the empty cooker base to Sauté mode and heat the passion fruit pulp. Stir in the whiskey, maple syrup, star anise, and chives. Cover with the Instant Pot Duo Crisp Air Fryer Lid and set to the Broil Smart Program for 6 minutes at 360°F. Set aside.
2. Rub the chicken with salt and black pepper, then transfer to the air fryer basket, cover with the Instant Pot Duo Crisp Air Fryer Lid.
3. Select the Air Fry Smart Program.
4. Divide the chicken into equal portions and drizzle with the chicken sauce.
5. Serve.

Nutritional value per serving:

Calories: 374kcal, Fat: 8g, Carbs: 34g, Protein: 37g

Duck and Plum Sauce

The duck is cooked with the plum sauce to improve the rate of absorption. Every bite of this lovely delicacy drips with deliciousness.
Prep time and cooking time: 40 minutes| Serves: 2

Ingredients To Use:

- 2 duck breasts
- 1 Tbsp. butter, melted
- star anise
- 1 Tbsp. olive oil
- 1 shallot, chopped
- 9 ounces red plumps, stoned, cut into small wedges
- 2 Tbsp. sugar

- 2 Tbsp. red wine
- 1 cup of beef stock

Step-by-Step Directions to Cook It:

1. Set the empty cooker base to Sauté mode and heat the oil. Stir in the shallot and fry for 5 minutes.
2. Add the plums and sugar. Heat until the sugar dissolves.
3. Add the wine and stock, cook for another 15 minutes, then transfer the contents to a bowl. Set aside.
4. Season the duck with salt and black pepper, rub with the melted butter, then transfer to an oven-safe baking dish that fits the Instant Pot cooker base.
5. Add the star anise and plum sauce, then cover with the Instant Pot Duo Crisp Air Fryer Lid. Set the Air Fry Smart Program for 12 minutes at 360°F.
6. Divide into equal portions and serve immediately.

Nutritional value per serving:

Calories: 400kcal, Fat: 25g, Carbs: 29g, Protein: 44g

Cajun chicken

This Cajun chicken is perfectly coated with Cajun spice then air fried making the boring chicken breasts interesting to eat
Prep Time and Cooking Time: 25 minutes| Serves: 2

Ingredients to use:
- 2 chicken breasts, boneless and skinless
- 3 tbsp. Cajun spice

Step-by-step Directions to Cook It:

1. Generously season the chicken breasts with the spice on both sides.
2. Place the dehydrating tray in the multilevel air fry basket then place the basket in the instant pot.
3. Arrange the chicken in the tray.
4. Seal the instant pot with an air fryer lid and set the temperature at 350°F and timer for 15 minutes on the air fryer setting.
5. Sere and enjoy

Nutritional value per serving:

Calories: 277kcal, Carbs: 0g Fat: 10.8g, Protein: 42.4g

Tasty Chicken tenders

Here is what you need! Delicious chicken tenders served with your favorite dip. These tenders will leave everyone with two thumbs up.
Prep Time and Cooking Time: 28 minutes| Serves: 4

Ingredients to use:
- 2 tbsp. sesame oil
- 6 tbsp. pineapple juice
- 2 tbsp. soy sauce

- 1 tbsp. ginger, minced
- 4 garlic cloves, minced
- 1 lb. chicken tenders

1. Add all ingredients in a bowl except the chicken tenders. Mix until well combined.
2. Add the chicken tenders and mix until well coated. Cover and refrigerate for 2 hours.
3. Place the dehydrating tray in the multilevel air fry basket then place the basket in the instant pot.
4. Place the marinated chicken tenders in the tray.
5. Seal the instant pot with an air fryer lid and select the air fryer mode. Set temperature to 350°F and the timer for 18 minutes.
6. When the chicken is halfway cooked, turn. Enjoy.

Calories: 298kcal, Carbs: 4.9g Fat: 15.3g, Protein: 33.6g

Chicken Casserole

This chicken casserole makes a healthy, satisfying weeknight dinner. The leftovers can be served for breakfast
Prep Time and Cooking Time: 35 minutes| Serves: 8

- 2 lb. chicken, cooked and shredded
- 6 oz. ham, cut into small pieces
- 4 oz. butter, melted
- 1 oz. lemon juice, fresh
- 1 tbsp. Dijon mustard
- 6 oz. cream cheese, softened
- 1/2 tbsp. salt
- 5 oz. Swiss cheese

1. Spray the instant pot inside with cooking spray.
2. Add chicken and ham to the instant pot. Spread them evenly.
3. Add butter, lemon juice, Dijon mustard, salt in a blender. Blend until smooth.
4. Spread the sauce over the chicken and ham then arrange the cheese slices on top.
5. Seal the instant pot with air fryer lid and select bake mode. Set temperature to 350°F and timer for 25 minutes. Serve and enjoy.

Calories: 231kcal, Carbs: 8.1g Fat: 15.7g, Protein: 15.4g

Baked Chicken and mushrooms

This is my favorite fast a healthy chicken recipe. The fresh mushrooms make the chicken

53

special enough to be served at a dinner party.

Prep Time and Cooking Time: 40 minutes| Serves: 2

Ingredients to use:

- 2 chicken breasts, boneless and skinless
- 1/4 cup mayonnaise
- 1/4 cup tomatoes, sun-dried
- 4 oz. mushrooms, sliced
- 1/2 tbsp. salt

Step-by-step Directions to Cook It:

1. Line the instant pot multilevel air fryer basket with foil.
2. Brush the chicken breasts with mayo then place them in the basket. Place the basket in the instant pot.
3. Add tomatoes, salt on the chicken.
4. Seal the instant pot with the air fryer lid and select the bake mode. Set temperature to 380^{0}F and timer for 30 minutes.
5. Serve when hot and enjoy.

Nutritional value per serving:

Calories: 408kcal, Carbs: 9.8g Fat: 20.8g, Protein: 44.5g

Easy Tarragon Chicken

This easy to make creamy tarragon chicken is delicious when served with mashed potatoes, cooked rice or pasta

Prep Time and Cooking Time: 22 minutes| Serves: 2

Ingredients to use:

- 2 chicken breasts, skinless and boneless
- 1 tbsp. butter, melted
- 2 tbsp. tarragon, dried
- 1/4 tbsp. garlic power
- Salt and pepper

Step-by-step Directions to Cook It:

1. Brush the chicken with butter the rub with tarragon, garlic, pepper.
2. Place the chicken in the dehydrating tray and place the tray in the multilevel air fryer basket. Place the basket in the instant pot.
3. Seal the instant pot with an air fryer lid and select air fryer mode. Set temperature to 390^{0}F and timer for 12 minutes.
4. Turn the chicken breasts when halfway cooked.
5. Serve when hot.

Nutritional value per serving:

Calories: 335kcal, Carbs: 1.2g Fat: 16.7g, Protein: 42.8g

Breaded Turkey Breast

This is the best way to enjoy turkey any time of the year. Breaded turkey is delicious, easy to make, pocket friendly and perfect for intimate

meals
Prep Time and Cooking Time: 25
minutes| Serves: 2

Ingredients to use:

- 1/4 tbsp. cayenne
- 1/4 tbsp. garlic powder
- 1/2 cup breadcrumbs
- Salt and pepper
- 1 turkey breast, skinless and boneless
- 3 tbsp. butter, melted

Step-by-step Directions to Cook It:

1. In a mixing bowl, mix cayenne, garlic powder, breadcrumbs, and pepper.
2. Brush the turkey with melted butter then coat with the breadcrumbs mixture.
3. Place the turkey in a dehydrating tray in the multilevel air fryer basket. Place the basket in the instant pot.
4. Seal the instant pot with an air fryer lid and select the air fryer function. Set temperature to 390⁰Fand time for 15 minutes.
5. Serve and enjoy

Nutritional value per serving:

Calories: 54kcal, Carbs: 9g Fat: -g, Protein: -g

Turkey Patties

These golden brown and super crispy turkey patties are a great way to make use of leftover turkey. The patties can be served on their own or in sandwiches.
Prep Time and Cooking Time: 35 minutes| Serves: 8

Ingredients to use:

- 1 egg, beaten lightly
- 2 tbsp. lemon juice
- 2 tbsp. cilantro, chopped
- 1 lb. ground turkey
- 1/3 cup breadcrumbs
- 1/2 tbsp. garlic, minced
- Salt and pepper

Step-by-step Directions to Cook It:

1. Add all the ingredients in a mixing bowl and mix until well combined.
2. Place the dehydrating tray in the air fryer basket then place the basket in the instant pot.
3. Use your hands to make small patties from the mixture. Place the patties in the dehydrating tray.
4. Seal the instant pot with an air fryer lid and select the bake function. Set temperature to 380⁰F and the timer for 25 minutes.
5. Turn the patties when halfway cooked. Serve.

Nutritional value per serving:

Calories: 138kcal, Carbs: 3.4g Fat: 7g, Protein: 16.9g

Italian Chicken Breast

This super Italian chicken breast is moist and packed with delicious flavor. Its a crowd please dish that everyone will love.

Prep Time and Cooking Time: 25 minutes| Serves: 1

Ingredients to use:

- 1 chicken breast, skinless and boneless
- 1 tbsp. olive oil
- 1 tbsp. Italian seasoning
- 1 tbsp. garlic, minced
- Salt and pepper

Step-by-step Directions to Cook It:

1. Coat the chicken breast with oil then rub wit seasoning, garlic, and pepper.
2. Place the dehydrating tray in the air fryer basket then place the basket in the instant pot.
3. Place chicken in the tray. Cover the instant pot with an air fryer lid.
4. Select an air fry setting and set the temperature to 380⁰F and time for 15 minutes.
5. Turn the chicken when halfway cooked. Serve and enjoy.

Nutritional value per serving:

Calories: 295kcal, Carbs: 2.5g Fat: 21g, Protein: 24g

Italian Chicken Thighs

The Italian air fryer chicken thighs pack a flavorful punch. They are easy to prepare and cook busy weeknight meal.

Prep Time and Cooking Time: 30 minutes| Serves: 4

Ingredients to use:

- 4 chicken thighs
- 2 tbsp. butter, melted
- 2 tbsp. Italian Herbs, dried
- 1/2 tbsp. garlic powder
- 1/4 tbsp. onion powder

Step-by-step Directions to Cook It:

1. Brush the chicken thighs with butter then rub with herbs, garlic, and onion powder.
2. Spray multilevel air fryer basket with cooking spray and insert it in the instant pot.
3. Place the chicken thighs in the basket. Seal the instant pot with the air fryer lid and select the air fry function.
4. Set temperature to 380⁰F and timer for 20 minutes.
5. Serve and enjoy.

Nutritional value per serving:

Calories: 336kcal, Carbs: 1.2g Fat: 16.9g, Protein: 42.5g

Flavorful Chicken Skewers

These chicken skewers are absolutely delicious, tender, and flavorful chicken that everyone will enjoy having during snacktime.
Prep Time and Cooking Time: 30 minutes| Serves: 4

Ingredients to use:

- 1-1/2 lb. chicken breast, cut into cube

Marinade

- 1/4 cup mint leaves, fresh
- 5 garlic cloves
- 1/2 cup lemon juice
- 1/4 tbsp. cayenne
- 1 tbsp. vinegar
- 1/2 cup yogurt
- 2 tbsp. rosemary, freshly chopped
- 2 tbsp. oregano
- Salt and pepper

Step-by-step Directions to Cook It:

1. Add all the marinade ingredients and blend until smooth. Pour the marinade in a mixing bowl.
2. Add the chicken to the bowl and mix it until good coated. Refrigerate for 1 hour.
3. Thread the chicken cubes onto soaked skewers. Spray the instant pot air fryer basket with cooking spray.
4. Place the skewers in the basket and place the basket in the instant pot.
5. Seal the instant pot with an air fryer lid and select the air fryer function.
6. Set temperature for 400⁰F and the timer for 20 minutes. Turn the skewers when halfway cooked.
7. Serve and enjoy when hot.

Nutritional value per serving:

Calories: 677kcal, Carbs: 7.1g Fat: 55.8g, Protein: 38.8g

Lemon Pepper Chicken

Flavorful and tender lemon pepper chicken is simple to bring together and can be served on its own or on vegetables and fried rice
Prep Time and Cooking Time: 45 minutes| Serves: 4

Ingredients to use:

- 4 chicken thighs
- 2 tbsp. lemon juice, fresh
- 2 tbsp. olive oil
- 1 tbsp. lemon pepper seasoning
- 1/2 tbsp. paprika
- 1/2 tbsp. Italian seasoning
- 1/2 tbsp. onion powder
- 1/2 tbsp. garlic powder
- 1 tbsp. salt

Step-by-step Directions to Cook It:

1. Add chicken thighs in a mixing bowl.

2. Mix lemon juice and olive oil in a separate bowl. Pour the mixture over the chicken thighs.
3. Mix lemon pepper seasoning, paprika, Italian seasoning, onion powder, garlic powder, salt, and pepper in another bowl. Rub the mixture on the chicken.
4. Spray your instant pot multilevel basket with cooking spray then add the chicken.
5. Place the basket in the instant pot and seal with the air fryer lid. Select the bake function.
6. Set temperature to 380^0F and timer for 35 minutes. Serve and enjoy.

Nutritional value per serving:

Calories: 349kcal, Carbs: 2.2g Fat: 18.1g, Protein: 42.7g

Chicken Fritters

If you love simple chicken recipes, then these fritters are the ones for you. They are easy yet packed with flavors.
Prep Time and Cooking Time: 20 minutes| Serves: 4

Ingredients to use:

- 1 lb. chicken, ground
- 1/2 tbsp. onion powder
- 1/2 tbsp. garlic powder
- 1/2 cup parmesan cheese, shredded
- 1/2 tbsp. dill, chopped

- 1/2 cup breadcrumbs
- 2 tbsp. green onion, chopped
- Salt and pepper

Step-by-step Directions to Cook It:

1. Add all ingredients in a mixing bowl and mix until well combined.
2. Place the dehydrating tray in the multi-level air fryer basket. Place the basket in the instant pot.
3. Make patties using the meat mixture while placing them in the tray.
4. Seal the instant pot using the air fryer lid and select the air fry function. Set temperature to 350^0F and the timer for 10 minutes.
5. Serve and enjoy.

Nutritional value per serving:

Calories: 309kcal, Carbs: 11.1g Fat: 11.1g, Protein: 38.5g

Easy Crisp Chicken Wings

Chicken wings are so delicious and easy to make that you will want to make them every time. Be sure to serve them with your favorite sauce for a filling dish
Prep Time and Cooking Time: 38 minutes| Serves: 3

Ingredients to use:

- 1/2 cup chicken stock
- 12 chicken wings
- 1/4 cup butter, melted

- Salt and pepper

1. Pour the chicken stock in the instant pot and place the steamer rack inside.
2. Place the chicken wings on the rack and seal the instant pot. Cook on high pressure for 8 minutes then release pressure quickly.
3. Remove the chicken wings from the instant pot and clean the pot.
4. Toss the chicken wings with butter then season with salt and pepper. Place the chicken wings in the air fryer basket. Place the basket in the instant pot.
5. Seal the instant pot with an air fryer lid and select the air fry function. Set the temperature to 400⁰F and the time for 10 minutes.
6. Air fry the chicken wings for 5-10 minutes. Serve and enjoy.

Calories: 784kcal, Carbs: 0.2g Fat: 40.7g, Protein: 98.7

Creamy Chicken Thighs

This creamy chicken is so awesome that it will make everyone wander in the kitchen with their nose high searching for what smells so delicious.

Prep Time and Cooking Time: 35 minutes| Serves: 6

- 1 tbsp. olive oil
- 6 chicken thighs, skin and bone-in
- Salt
- Black pepper, freshly ground
- 2 garlic cloves, minced
- 1 tbsp. thyme leaves, fresh
- 1 tbsp. red pepper flakes, crushed
- 3/4 cup chicken broth, low sodium
- 1/2 cup heavy cream
- 1/2 cup sundried tomatoes, chopped
- 1/4 cup parmesan cheese, grated
- Basil for serving, freshly torn

1. Set your instant pot to sauté function.
2. Stir in oil, chicken, salt, and pepper. Sear the chicken for 5 minutes on each side.
3. Add garlic, thyme, pepper flakes, broth, heavy cream, tomatoes, and cheese to the instant pot. Stir well to coat the chicken.
4. Seal the instant pot with the air fryer lid and select the bake function. Set temperature at 350⁰F and timer at 20 minutes.
5. Garnish with basil and serve. Enjoy.

Calories: 454kcal, Carbs: 2.8g Fat: 37.8g, Protein: 26.9g

Turkey Tenderloin skewers

This is a brilliant and easy dinner option for any day. These turkey skewers require few ingredients and less time to make
Prep Time and Cooking Time: 24 minutes| Serves: 1

Ingredients to use:

- 1-1/2 lb. turkey tenderloin, cut into 1" cubes
- Salt and pepper
- 2 tbsp. garlic, minced
- 1 tbsp. Italian seasoning, salt-free
- 2 tbsp. olive oil
- skewers

Step-by-step Directions to Cook It:

1. Season the turkey with salt and pepper.
2. In a mixing bowl, mix garlic, seasoning, and oil until well mixed. Add the turkey pieces and mix until well coated.
3. Thread the turkey cubes to the skewers and place them in the air fryer basket. Put the basket in the instant pot and seal the instant pot with the air fryer lid.
4. Set temperature to 350⁰F and timer for 14 minutes. When its half cooked turn the turkey

skewers.
5. Serve with your favorite sauce.

Nutritional value per serving:

Calories: 316kcal, Carbs: 1g Fat: 10g, Protein: 51g

Simple Spiced Chicken Legs

These simple spiced chicken legs are juicy and flavorful. Coated with salt, pepper, garlic powder and paprika.
Prep time and cooking time: 30 minutes | Serves: 6

Ingredients To Use:

- 2-2.5 lbs. chicken drumsticks 6-8 legs
- 2 tbsp. olive oil
- 1 tsp. kosher salt
- 1 tsp. pepper
- 1 tsp. garlic powder
- 1 tsp. smoked paprika
- 1/2 tsp. cumin

Step-by-Step Directions to cook it:

1. Take a large bowl and drizzle the drumsticks with olive oil and toss them to coat.
2. Take a small bowl, stir together the remaining ingredients followed by sprinkling over drumsticks and toss to coat evenly.
3. Divide the coated chicken onto cooking trays of the Instant Pot Duo Crisp Air Fryer.
4. Select Air Fry from the display

panel, then adjust the temperature to 400°F and the time to 25 minutes, touch the start button.

5. Once preheated, insert two cooking trays in the top-most position and in the bottom-most position one in each.
6. After half time, turn the food over and switch the cooking trays between the top and bottom positions.
7. When the Air Fryer program is complete, check to make sure the thickest portion of the meat reads at least 165°F.
8. Remove and serve hot.

Calories 222, Fat 14g, Carbs 1g, Protein 23g

Herb-Roasted Turkey Breast

Best idea for thanksgiving dinner. This herb roasted turkey breast is a delicious and flavorful.
Prep time and cooking time: 70 minutes | Serves: 8

Ingredients To Use:

- 3 lb. turkey breast

Rub Ingredients

- 2 tbsp. olive oil
- 2 tbsp. lemon juice
- 1 tbsp. minced Garlic
- 2 tsp. ground mustard
- 2 tsp. kosher salt
- 1 tsp. pepper
- 1 tsp. dried rosemary
- 1 tsp. dried thyme
- 1 tsp. ground sage

Step-by-Step Directions to cook it:

1. Take a small bowl and thoroughly combine the Rub Ingredients in it. Rub this on the outside of the turkey breast and under any loose skin.
2. Place the coated turkey breast keeping skin side up on a cooking tray.
3. Place the drip pan at the bottom of the cooking chamber of the Instant Pot Duo Crisp Air Fryer. Select Air Fry option, post this, adjust the temperature to 360°F and the time to one hour, then touch start.
4. When preheated, add the food to the cooking tray in the lowest position. Close the lid for cooking.
5. When the Air Fry program is complete, check to make sure that the thickest portion of the meat reads at least 160°F, remove the turkey and let it rest for 10 minutes before slicing and serving.

Calories 222, Fat 14g, Carbs 1g, Protein 23g

Fried Whole Chicken

A Fried Chicken for a whole family. Easy to prepare and easy to cook. Let the air fryer do the magic!
Prep time and cooking time: 75 minutes | Serves: 4

Ingredients To Use:

- 1 Whole chicken
- 2 Tbsp. or spray of oil of choice
- 1 tsp. garlic powder
- 1 tsp. onion powder
- 1 tsp. paprika
- 1 tsp. Italian seasoning
- 2 Tbsp. Montreal Steak Seasoning (or salt and pepper to taste)
- 1.5 cup chicken broth

Step-by-Step Directions to cook it:

1. Truss and wash the chicken.
2. Mix the seasoning and rub a little amount on the chicken.
3. Pour the broth inside the Instant Pot Duo Crisp Air Fryer.
4. Place the chicken in the air fryer basket.
5. Select the option Air Fry and Close the Air Fryer lid and cook for 25 minutes.
6. Spray or rub the top of the chicken with oil and rub it with half of the seasoning.
7. Close the air fryer lid and air fry again at 400°F for 10 minutes.
8. Flip the chicken, spray it with oil, and rub with the remaining seasoning.
9. Again air fry it for another ten minutes.
10. Allow the chicken to rest for 10 minutes.

Nutrition Facts Per Serving:

Calories 436, Fat 28g, Carbs 4g, Protein 42g

Barbecue Air Fried Chicken

These barbecue air fried chicken is good for summer. Just marinate it with seasoning and put it in the air fryer. Tasty and delicious.
Prep time and cooking time: 31 minutes | Serves 10

Ingredients To Use:

- 1 teaspoon Liquid Smoke
- 2 cloves Fresh Garlic smashed
- 1/2 cup Apple Cider Vinegar
- 3 pounds Chuck Roast well-marbled with intramuscular fat
- 1 Tablespoon Kosher Salt
- 1 Tablespoon Freshly Ground Black Pepper
- 2 teaspoons Garlic Powder
- 1.5 cups Barbecue Sauce
- 1/4 cup Light Brown Sugar + more for sprinkling
- 2 Tablespoons Honey optional and in place of 2 TBL sugar

Step-by-Step Directions to cook it:

1. Add meat to the Instant Pot Duo

Crisp Air Fryer Basket, spreading out the meat.
2. Select the option Air Fry.
3. Close the Air Fryer lid and cook at 300 degrees F for 8 minutes. Pause the Air Fryer and flip meat over after 4 minutes.
4. Remove the lid and baste with more barbecue sauce and sprinkle with a little brown sugar.
5. Again Close the Air Fryer lid and set the temperature at 400°F for 9 minutes. Watch meat though the lid and flip it over after 5 minutes.

Nutrition Facts Per Serving:

Calories 360, Fat 16g, Carbs 27g, Protein 27g

Boneless Air Fryer Turkey Breasts

Boneless air fryer turkey breast is so easy to make. This juicy turkey breast is so beautiful you can make it in less than an hour.
Prep time and cooking time: 60 minutes | Serves 4

Ingredients To Use:

- 3 lbs. turkey breast, boneless
- 1/4 cup mayonnaise
- 1/2 tsp. garlic powder
- 2 tsps. poultry seasoning
- Black pepper and salt to taste

Step-by-Step Directions to cook it:

1. Choose the Air Fry option on the Instant Pot Duo Crisp Air fryer. Set the temperature to 360°F and push start. The preheating will start.
2. Apply all the seasonings to your boneless turkey breast.
3. Once preheated, Air Fry the turkey breasts on 360°F for about 1 hour. Ensure you turn after every 15 minutes or until you have an internal temperature of 165°F.

Nutrition Facts Per Serving:

Calories 558, Fat 18g, Carbs 1g, Protein 98g

BBQ Chicken Breasts

Tender, juicy chicken and grilled to perfection. Marinated in barbecue seasonings to have a better taste.
Prep time and cooking time: 20 minutes | Serves 4

Ingredients To Use:

- 4 chicken breasts (6 oz. each), boneless and skinless
- 2 tbsps. bbq seasoning
- Olive oil

Step-by-Step Directions to cook it:

1. Apply the BBQ seasoning to both sides of chicken breasts. Cover

the chicken breasts and set in a refrigerator to marinate for about 45 minutes.

2. Choose the Air Fry option and set the temperature to 400°F. Push start and let it preheat for 5 minutes.
3. Upon preheating, place the chicken breast in the basket of the Instant Pot Duo Crisp Air Fryer. They should not overlap. Use olive oil to spray over the breasts.
4. Cook for around 14 minutes. Flip halfway.
5. The internal temperature should be 160°F. Place on a plate and allow to cool for about 5 minutes before you slice.

Calories 131, Fat 3g, Carbs 2g, Protein 24g

Juicy Turkey Burgers

The juiciest and most delicious burger. Simple to make on the grill or stovetop. Perfect for watching movies!
Prep time and cooking time: 30 minutes | Serves 8

Ingredients To Use:

- 1 lb. ground turkey 85% lean / 15% fat
- 1/4 cup unsweetened apple sauce
- 1/2 onion grated
- 1 Tbsp. ranch seasoning
- 2 tsp. Worcestershire Sauce
- 1 tsp. minced garlic
- 1/4 cup plain breadcrumbs
- Salt and pepper to taste

Step-by-Step Directions to cook it:

1. Combine the onion, ground turkey, unsweetened apple sauce, minced garlic, breadcrumbs, ranch seasoning, Worchestire sauce, and salt and pepper. Mix them with your hands until well combined. Form 4 equally sized hamburger patties with them.
2. Place these burgers in the refrigerator for about 30 minutes to have them firm up a bit.
3. While preparing for cooking, select the Air Fry option. Set the temperature of 360°F and the cook time as required. Press start to begin preheating.
4. Once the preheating temperature is reached, place the burgers on the tray in the Air fryer basket, making sure they don't overlap or touch. Cook on for 15 minutes, flipping halfway through.

Nutrition Facts Per Serving:

Calories 183, Fat 3g, Carbs 11g, Protein 28g

Turkey Legs

Serve with dressing, noodles or rice. This turkey legs can also be increased very easily.
Prep time and cooking time: 45 mins | Serves 2

Ingredients To Use:

- 2 turkey legs
- 1-1/2 tsps. Paprika, smoked
- 1 tsp. sugar, brown
- 1 tsp. salt
- 1/2 tsp. garlic powder
- Avocado oil for spraying.

Step-by-Step Directions to cook it:

1. Mix the paprika, sugar, salt, and garlic powder.
2. Wash the turkey legs and pat dry using a paper towel.
3. Rub the seasoning mixture on the turkey legs. Ensure you apply under the skin.
4. While preparing for cooking, select the Air Fry option. Press start to begin preheating.
5. Once the preheating temperature is reached, place the turkey legs on the tray in the basket of the Instant Pot Duo Crisp Air Fryer. Spray them lightly with oil.
6. Air Fry the turkey legs for 20 minutes at 400°F. Open the Air Fryer lid and flip the turkey legs and spray lightly with avocado oil.

Close the Instant Pot Duo Crisp Air Fryer lid and cook for 20 minutes more.
7. Divide in plates and Enjoy.

Nutrition Facts Per Serving:

Calories 958, Fat 46g, Carbs 3g, Protein 133g

Honey Garlic Chicken Drumsticks

These honey garlic chicken drumsticks is full of flavor, perfect for an easy weeknight meal!
Prep Time and cooking time: 22 minutes | Serve: 2

Ingredients To Use:

- 2 chicken drumsticks
- 1 tsp. honey
- 1/2 tbsp. olive oil
- 1/2 tsp. garlic paste
- 1/2 tsp. mustard
- Pepper
- Salt

Step-by-Step Directions to cook it:

1. Add all ingredients to the large bowl and mix well.
2. Place the dehydrating tray in a multi-level air fryer basket and place basket in the instant pot.
3. Place chicken on the dehydrating tray.
4. Seal pot with air fryer lid and select air fry mode then set the

temperature to 350 F and timer for 12 minutes. Turn chicken halfway through.
5. Serve and enjoy.

Nutritional value per serving:

Calories 123 Fat 6.4 g Carbs 3.4 g Protein 12.9 g

Flavors Southwest Chicken

Packed with texture, bright flavors, and awesome colors. These southwest chicken is tasty and delicious!
Prep Time and cooking time: 35 minutes | Serve: 2

Ingredients To Use:

- 1/2 lb. chicken breasts, skinless and boneless
- 1/4 tsp. chili powder
- 1/2 tbsp. olive oil
- 1 tbsp. lime juice
- 1/8 tsp. garlic powder
- 1/8 tsp. onion powder
- 1/4 tsp. cumin
- 1/8 tsp. salt

Step-by-Step Directions to cook it:

1. Add all ingredients into the zip-lock bag and shake well and place it in the refrigerator for 1 hour.
2. Place the dehydrating tray in a multi-level air fryer basket and place basket in the instant pot.
3. Place marinated chicken wings on dehydrating tray.
4. Seal pot with air fryer lid and select air fry mode then set the temperature to 400 F and timer for 25 minutes. Turn chicken halfway through.
5. Serve and enjoy.

Nutritional value per serving:

Calories 254 Fat 12 g Carbs 2.4 g Protein 33 g

Chapter 5: Seafood Recipes

Instant Air Fried Branzino

With the Instant Pot Duo Crisp Air Fryer Lid, this recipe results in crispy, crunchy delicious branzino fillets.
Prep time and cooking time: 20 minutes| Serves: 4

Ingredients To Use:

- 1 lemon, zested and grated
- A pinch of red pepper flakes, crushed
- 1 orange, zested and grated
- 1/2 lemon, juiced
- 1/2 orange, juiced
- 4 medium branzino fillets, boneless
- 1/2 cup of parsley, chopped
- 2 Tbsp. olive oil
- Salt and black pepper, as desired

Step-by-Step Directions to Cook It:

1. Mix the fish fillets, orange and lemon zest, lemon and orange juice, salt, black pepper, pepper flakes, and oil in a large bowl.
2. Transfer the coated fillets to the air fryer basket and cover with the Instant Pot Duo Crisp Air Fryer Lid. Select the Air Fry Smart program and set the timer for 10 minutes at 350°F.

3. Turn the food when directed to by the Lid.
4. Divide the fish into equal portions and serve immediately.

Nutritional value per serving:

Calories: 261kcal, Fat: 8g, Carbs: 21g, Protein: 12g

Marinated Salmon

This salmon is infused with taste during the 1 hour that it is kept in the fridge. Air frying the marinated salmon will result in a crispy and tasty meal.
Prep time and cooking time: 1 hour 20 minutes | Serves: 6

Ingredients To Use:

- 1 whole salmon
- 1 Tbsp. dill, chopped
- 1 Tbsp. tarragon, chopped
- 1 Tbsp. garlic, minced
- 2 lemons, juiced
- 1 lemon, sliced
- A pinch of salt and black pepper

Step-by-Step Directions to Cook It:

1. Season the fish with the salt, black pepper, and lemon juice. Keep in the refrigerator for 1 hour to marinate.

2. Stuff the salmon with the lemon and garlic slices, transfer to the air fryer basket, and cover with the Instant Pot Duo Crisp Air Fryer Lid. Select the Air Fry Smart Program and cook for 25 minutes at 320°F.
3. Divide into equal portions and serve immediately. Serve with coleslaw.

Nutritional value per serving:

Calories: 300kcal, Fat: 8g, Carbs: 19g, Protein: 27g

Hawaiian Salmon

Are you in the mood for a well-seasoned, crunchy, and crispy fish meal? Then this is the perfect recipe for you.
Prep time and cooking time: 20 minutes | Serves: 2

Ingredients To Use:

- 20 ounces of canned pineapple pieces and juice
- 1/2 tsp. ginger, grated
- 2 tsp. garlic powder
- 1 tsp. onion powder
- 1 Tbsp. balsamic vinegar
- 2 medium salmon fillets, boneless
- Salt and black pepper, as desired

Step-by-Step Directions to Cook It:

1. Season the salmon with the

garlic, onion, salt, and pepper.
2. Transfer the seasoned salmon to an oven-safe baking dish that fits into the Instant Pot cooker base.
3. Drizzle the salmon with vinegar and cover with the Instant Pot Duo Crisp Air Fryer Lid. Select the Air Fry Smart Program and set the timer for 10 minutes at 350°F.
4. Divide into equal portions and serve immediately.

Nutritional value per serving:

Calories: 200kcal, Fat: 8g, Carbs: 17g, Protein: 20g

Chinese Cod

This recipe is perfect for lovers of Chinese flavor. The cod is adequately seasoned with ginger and soy sauce.
Prep time and cooking time: 20 minutes| Serves: 2

Ingredients To Use:

- 1 2 medium cod fillets, boneless
- 1 tsp. peanuts, crushed
- 2 tsp. garlic powder
- 1 Tbsp. light soy sauce
- 1/2 tsp. ginger, grated

Step-by-Step Directions to Cook It:

1. Place the cod fillets in the oven-safe baking dish and season with garlic, soy sauce, and ginger.
2. Transfer to the Instant Pot

cooker base and cover with the Instant Pot Duo Crisp Air Fryer Lid and select the Air Fry Smart Program.
3. Set the timer for 10 minutes at 350°F.
4. Divide into equal portions and sprinkle with peanuts.

Calories: 254kcal, Fat: 10g, Carbs: 14g, Protein: 23g

Halibut and Sun-Dried Tomatoes Mix

The Halibut is coated with sun-dried tomatoes and air fried for delicious, crunchy goodness.
Prep time and cooking time: 20 minutes | Serves: 2

Ingredients To Use:

- 2 medium halibut fillets
- 2 garlic cloves, minced
- 2 tsp. olive oil
- Salt and black pepper, as desired
- 6 sun-dried tomatoes, chopped
- 2 small red onions, sliced
- 1 fennel bulb, sliced
- 9 black olives, pitted and sliced
- 4 rosemary springs, chopped
- 1/2 tsp. red pepper flakes, crushed

Step-by-Step Directions to Cook It:

1. Coat the halibut fillets with the salt, pepper, garlic, and oil. Transfer to an oven-safe baking dish that fits into the Instant Pot cooker base.
2. Add the onion slices, tomatoes, olives, fennel, pepper flakes, and rosemary.
3. Transfer the dish to the air fryer, add the dehydration tray, and cover with the Instant Pot Duo Crisp Air Fryer Lid.
4. Select the Air Fry Smart Program and set the timer for 10 minutes at 380°F.
5. Divide the fish and vegetables among plates and serve.

Nutritional value per serving:

Calories: 213kcal, Fat: 12g, Carbs: 23g, Protein: 17g

Stuffed Calamari

Whether fresh, frozen, large, or small calamari, this recipe works for all. Enjoy this lovely recipe with the Instant Pot Duo Crisp Air Fryer Lid.
Prep time and cooking time: 35 minutes | Serves: 4

Ingredients To Use:

- 4 big calamari, tentacles separated and chopped and tubes reserved
- 2 Tbsp. parsley, chopped
- 5 ounces kale, chopped
- 2 garlic cloves, minced
- 1 red bell pepper, chopped

- 1 Tbsp. olive oil
- 2 ounces canned tomato puree
- 1 yellow onion, chopped
- Salt and black pepper, as desired

1. Set the empty cooker base to Sauté mode and heat the oil. Stir in the garlic and onion—Fry for about 2 minutes.
2. Add the bell peppers, calamari tentacles, salt, pepper, tomato puree, and kale. Stir and cook for 10 minutes.
3. Transfer the contents of the air fryer to a bowl.
4. Stuff the calamari with the tomato puree mixture and hold with toothpicks.
5. Transfer the calamari to the air fryer, cover with the Instant Pot Duo Crisp Air Fryer Lid, and select the Air Fry Smart Program.
6. Set the timer for 20 minutes at 360°F.
7. Divide into equal portions and sprinkle with parsley. Serve.

Nutritional value per serving:

Calories: 322kcal, Fat: 10g, Carbs: 14g, Protein: 22g

Crusted Salmon

You can get cooked salmons everywhere, at the store, restaurant, or even in your own home. With the Instant Pot Duo Crisp Air Fryer Lid, you can make restaurant-worthy crusty salmon in your kitchen. Prep time and cooking time: 20 minutes | Serves: 4

Ingredients To Use:

- 1 cup of pistachios, chopped
- 4 salmon fillets
- 1/4 cup of lemon juice
- 2 Tbsp. honey
- 1 tsp. dill, chopped
- Salt and black pepper, as desired
- 1 Tbsp. mustard

Step-by-Step Directions to Cook It:

1. Mix the pistachios, honey, mustard, dill, salt, black pepper, and lemon juice in a bowl. This will serve as the rub.
2. Coat the salmon with the rub and transfer to the air fryer basket.
3. Cover the Instant Pot cooker base with Instant Pot Air Fryer Lid and set the Air Fry Smart Program.
4. Set the timer for 10 minutes at 350°F
5. Divide into equal portions and serve with salad.

Nutritional value per serving:

Calories: 300kcal, Fat: 17g, Carbs: 20g, Protein: 22g

Swordfish and Mango Salsa

The mango sauce adds a delicious fruitiness to the Instant Roasted Swordfish steaks. Ensure you eat each bite with the mango salsa.
Prep time and cooking time: 16 minutes | Serves: 2

- 2 medium swordfish steaks
- Salt and black pepper, as desired
- 2 tsp. avocado oil
- 1 Tbsp. cilantro, chopped
- 1 mango, chopped
- 1 avocado, pitted, peeled and chopped
- A pinch of cumin
- A pinch of onion powder
- A pinch of garlic powder
- 1 orange, peeled and sliced
- 1/2 Tbsp. balsamic vinegar

Step-by-Step Directions to Cook It:

1. Rub the swordfish with onion, garlic, pepper, salt, cumin, and black pepper.
2. Rub the seasoned steaks with 1/2 the oil and transfer to the Air Fryer basket.
3. Cover with the Instant Pot cooker base with the Instant Pot Duo Crisp Air Fryer Lid. Select the Roast Smart Program and set the timer to 6 minutes at 360°F.
4. Turn the food when directed by the appliance.

5. In a small bowl, mix the mango, avocado, cilantro, salt, vinegar, black pepper, and leftover oil.
6. Divide the roasted fish into equal portions and serve with the mango salsa and orange slices.

Nutritional value per serving:

Calories: 200kcal, Fat: 7g, Carbs: 14g, Protein: 14g

Squid and Guacamole

The squid is air fried and crunchy and then eaten with the delicious guacamole salad.
Prep time and cooking time: 20 minutes| Serves: 4

Ingredients To Use:

- 2 medium squids, tentacles separated and tubes scored lengthwise
- 1 Tbsp. olive oil
- Juice from 1 lime
- Salt and black pepper, as desired

Guacamole Ingredients:

- 2 avocados, pitted, peeled and chopped
- 1 Tbsp. coriander, chopped
- 2 red chilies, chopped
- 1 tomato, chopped
- 1 red onion, chopped
- 2 limes, juiced

Step-by-Step Directions to Cook It:

1. Season the squid and its

tentacles with the salt, black pepper, and drizzle with olive oil.

2. Transfer the seasoned squid to the air fryer basket and cover with the Instant Pot Duo Crisp Air Fryer Lid.
3. Select the Air Fry smart program and set the timer to 6 minutes and 360°F.
4. Remove the squid from the air fryer and drizzle with lime juice.
5. In a small bowl, mix the avocado, coriander, tomato, chilies, onion, and juice. Mash the ingredients together with a fork and stir well.
6. Serve the squids into plates and top with the guacamole.

Nutritional value per serving:

Calories: 260kcal, Fat: 7g, Carbs: 28g, Protein: 18g

Tuna and Chimichurri Sauce

The chimichurri sauce adds flavor and aroma to the arugula—the combination of the arugula and Tuna results in a fantastic combination. Prep time and cooking time: 18 minutes| Serves: 4

Ingredients To Use:

- 1/2 cup of cilantro, chopped
- 1/3 cup of olive oil+ 2 Tbsp.
- 1 small red onion, chopped
- 3 Tbsp. balsamic vinegar
- 2 Tbsp. parsley, chopped
- 2 Tbsp. basil, chopped
- 1 jalapeno pepper, chopped
- 1 pound of sushi tuna steak
- Salt and black pepper, as desired
- 1 tsp. red pepper flakes
- 1 tsp. thyme, chopped
- 3 garlic cloves, minced
- 2 avocados, pitted, peeled and sliced
- 6 ounces baby arugula

Step-by-Step Directions to Cook It:

1. Mix the jalapeno pepper, onion, vinegar, basil, cilantro, garlic, pepper flakes, parsley, thyme, salt, and black pepper in a small bowl. Set aside.
2. Season with the tuna with salt, pepper, and oil.
3. Transfer the seasoned tuna to the air fryer and cover with the Instant Pot Duo Crisp Air Fryer Lid.
4. Select the Bake Smart Program, and set the timer for 6 minutes at 360°F. Turn the food after 3 minutes.
5. Meanwhile, mix the arugula with 1/2 of the chimichurri mix prepared at the beginning. Toss vigorously to coat.
6. When ready, slice up the salmon.
7. Divide the arugula into two equal portions, add the sliced salmon, and top with the remnant of the chimichurri sauce.

8. Serve.

Nutritional value per serving:

Calories: 276kcal, Fat: 3g, Carbs: 14g, Protein: 20g

Potato Fish Cakes

This is a great idea for a weeknight dinner. It's packed with protein, it's filling, and every member of the family will love it.
Prep Time and Cooking Time: 25 minutes| Serves: 4

Ingredients to use:

- 2 cups white fish
- 1 tbsp. coriander
- 1 tbsp. Worcestershire sauce
- 2 tbsp. chili powder
- 1 cup potatoes, mashed
- 1 tbsp. mixed herbs
- 1 tbsp. mixed spice
- 1 tbsp. milk
- 1 tbsp. butter
- 1 small onion, diced
- 1/4 cup breadcrumbs
- Salt and pepper

Step-by-step Directions to Cook It:

1. Add all the ingredients in a mixing bowl and mix to combine.
2. Use your hands to make patties and refrigerate for 2 hours.
3. Place the patties in a dehydrating tray in the multilevel air fryer basket. Place the basket in the instant pot.

4. Seal the instant pot with an air fryer lid and select an air fry function. Set time to 400⁰F and the timer for 15 minutes.
5. Turn the patties when halfway cooked.
6. Serve and enjoy.

Nutritional value per serving:

Calories: 290kcal, Carbs: 13.8g Fat: 21.5g, Protein: 11.2g

Baked Cod Fillet

If looking for a delicious simple weeknight dinner for your coming over friends, then this Instant pot Air fry lid baked cod fillet is a solid choice for you.
Prep Time and Cooking Time: 30 minutes| Serves: 4

Ingredients to use:

- 1 lb. cod fillet
- 1 tbsp. olive oil
- 1 tbsp. Italian seasoning
- Salt and pepper
- Salt and pepper
- 1/4 cup olives.
- 1 cup cherry tomatoes, halved

Step-by-step Directions to Cook It:

1. Line your instant pot air fryer basket with parchment paper.
2. Coat the cod with oil and season with seasoning, salt, and pepper.
3. Place the fish in the basket then place the basket in the instant

pot. Place olives and tomatoes on the fish.

4. Seal the instant pot with an air fryer lid and select the air fry function. Set temperature to 400⁰F and the timer for 20 minutes.

5. Serve the fish immediately.

Nutritional value per serving:

Calories: 143kcal, Carbs: 2.4g Fat: 5.9g, Protein: 20.7g

Instant Pot Duo Crisp Air fryer Lid Fish

This fish is moist and soft from the inside and crispy on the outside. It is ready on your table even before you know it so perfect for busy times meals.

Prep Time and Cooking Time: 20 minutes| Serves: 8

Ingredients to use:

- 8 fish fillets
- 1 tbsp. olive oil
- 1 cup dried breadcrumbs
- 1/2 tbsp. paprika
- 1/4 tbsp. chili powder
- 1/4 tbsp. garlic powder
- 1/4 tbsp. onion powder
- 1/2 tbsp. salt
- 1/4 tbsp. black pepper

Step-by-step Directions to Cook It:

1. Drizzle olive oil on the fillets until well coated

2. In a mixing bowl, mix breadcrumbs, paprika, chili powder, garlic powder, onion powder, salt, and black pepper.

3. Coat the fish with the breadcrumb mixture and transfer it to the air fryer basket in the instant pot.

4. Seal the instant pot with an air fryer lid and select air fry mode. Set temperature to 390⁰F and the timer for 15 minutes. Flip the fillets when halfway cooked.

5. Serve when hot with your favorite sauce and enjoy it.

Nutritional value per serving:

Calories: 153kcal, Carbs: 11g Fat: 3g, Protein: 21g

Instant Pot Air fryer Lid Salmon

This salmon is just cooked to perfection. Seared edges with a soft and flaky center. this is a must-try recipe especially if you just purchased your Instant pot air fryer lid.

Prep Time and Cooking Time: 12 minutes| Serves: 1

Ingredients to use:

- 2 6oz salmon fillets
- 2 tbsp. olive oil
- 1 tbsp. paprika
- 1 tbsp. garlic powder
- 1 tbsp. onion powder

- Salt and pepper

1. Rub the salmon with olive oil until well coated.
2. In a mixing bowl, mix paprika, garlic powder, onion powder, salt, and pepper until well combined. Rub the spice mix on the salmon.
3. Place the salmon in the air fryer basket in the inner pot of the instant pot. Seal the instant pot with an air fryer lid.
4. Set temperature to 400^0F and the timer for 8 minutes. The internal temperature should reach 140^0.
5. Serve the salmon to your liking.

Nutritional value per serving:

Calories: 53kcal, Carbs: 3g Fat: 5g, Protein: 1g

Instant Pot Air fryer Lid Whole Fish

This is a finger-licking delicious, quick to make tender fish that the Instant pot Air fryer lid will cook within five minutes.
Prep Time and Cooking Time: 10 minutes| Serves: 2

Ingredients to use:

- 2 whole fish
- 1 tbsp. smoked paprika
- 1 tbsp. onion powder
- 1/2 tbsp. ginger
- 1 small stock cube
- 2 tbsp. vegetable oil
- 1 cup water
- Salt
- 1 tbsp. cayenne pepper

Step-by-step Directions to Cook It:

1. Clean and pat dry the fish with a paper towel. Make two slashes on the fish.
2. In a mixing bowl, mix paprika, onion powder, ginger, stock cube, oil, salt, and pepper.
3. Rub the marinade on the fish and ensure it's well coated.
4. Pour water in the instant pot and place a trivet. Cook on high for 4 minutes then release pressure quickly.
5. Take off the lid, remove the fish, and empty the inner pot. Clean it and dry it.
6. Place the fish in an air fryer basket and place the basket in the inner pot. Seal the instant pot with an air fryer lid.
7. Select the air fry function. Set temperature to 220^0F and the timer for 6 minutes.
8. Serve.

Nutritional value per serving:

Calories: 352kcal, Carbs: 3g Fat: 18g, Protein: 45g

Bacon-Wrapped Shrimp

These bacon-wrapped shrimp make an amazing snack, appetizer, or dinner. This is a big reason to buy an Instant pot air fryer lid.
Prep Time and Cooking Time: 25 minutes| Serves: 6

Ingredients to use:

- 8 oz. shrimp
- 1 tbsp. oil
- 1 tbsp. Cajun seasoning blend
- 8 slices center-cut bacon

Step-by-step Directions to Cook It:

1. Rub salmon generously with oil.
2. Cut the bacon into half both widthwise and lengthwise.
3. Wrap each piece of bacon around the shrimp and place the fish in the air fryer basket seam side down in a single layer.
4. Place the basket in the instant pot and seal it using an air fryer lid.
5. Set temperature to 370⁰F and the timer for 8 minutes. Flip the shrimp when halfway cooked.
6. Serve and enjoy.

Nutritional value per serving:

Calories: 181kcal, Carbs: -g Fat: 14g, Protein: 11g

Fish Sticks

To be honest, my first time to make these fish sticks was quite impressive. They are perfectly crispy on the outside while the inside is tender and flaky.
Prep Time and Cooking Time: 20 minutes| Serves: 4

Ingredients to use:

- 1 lb. cod fillet
- 1/4 cup all-purpose flour
- 1 egg
- 1/2 cup panko bread crumbs
- 1/4 cup parmesan cheese
- 1 tbsp. parsley flakes
- 1 tbsp. paprika
- 1/2 tbsp. black pepper
- Cooking spray

Step-by-step Directions to Cook It:

1. Pat dry the cod fillet with a paper towel.
2. Add flour in a mixing bowl. Beat eggs in a separate mixing bowl. Mix bread crumbs, cheese, parsley flakes, paprika, and black pepper in the third mixing bowl.
3. Coat each cot fillet with flour, then in eggs, and finally in the breadcrumbs mixture. Arrange them in a sprayed air fryer basket making sure they don't touch each other.
4. Place the basket in the instant

pot and seal with an air fryer lid.

5. Select air fry and set the temperature to 400⁰F and timer for 10 minutes. Flip the fish sticks when halfway cooked.

6. Serve with sauce and enjoy.

Nutritional value per serving:

Calories: 54kcal, Carbs: 9g Fat: -g, Protein: -g

Instant Pot Duo Crisp Air Fryer Lid Salmon with Dill Sauce

This is an incredibly low carb dish to whip up. The fish is cooked to perfection and the dill sauce throws the flavors to the top.
Prep Time and Cooking Time: 12 minutes| Serves: 4

Ingredients to use:

- 2 tbsp. oil
- 4 salmon fillets
- Salt and pepper
- 1/2 tbsp. paprika
- 1 lemon Zest and juice
- 1 tbsp. garlic
- 1/3 cup sour cream
- 1/3 cup mayonnaise
- 1/2 tbsp. English style mustard
- 3 tbsp. dill, fresh

Step-by-step Directions to Cook It:

1. Rub the salmon fillet with oil then season it.

2. Place the air fryer basket in the instant pot then place the salmon fillet in the basket.

3. Seal the instant pot with an air fryer lid. Select the air fry function.

4. Set temperature to 390⁰F and time for 7 minutes.

5. Meanwhile, mix lemon juice, garlic, sour cream, mayonnaise, mustard, and dill in a mixing bowl.

6. Serve the salmon topped with 3 tablespoons of the sauce. Enjoy.

Nutritional value per serving:

Calories: 702kcal, Carbs: 2g Fat: 53g, Protein: 51g

Lemon Garlic Salmon

Make this flavorful and deliciously crispy salmon packed with lemon and garlic withing 20 minutes. It's perfect for busy lunchtimes or dinner meal
Prep Time and Cooking Time: 16 minutes| Serves: 2

Ingredients to use:

- 4 6oz salmon fillets
- 2 tbsp. olive oil
- 1 tbsp. lemon juice
- 2 tbsp. Italian Herbs
- 2 tbsp. garlic powder
- 1 tbsp. Celtic salt
- 1 tbsp. cracked pepper, fresh
- 1 lemon, sliced into1 tbsp. lemon juice

1. Drizzle oil and lemon juice on the salmon fillet then season with Italian herbs, garlic, salt, and pepper.
2. Arrange the fillets on the air fryer basket ensuring they don't touch each other.
3. Arrange lemon slices on the salmon then seal the instant pot with air fryer lid. Select air fry setting.
4. Set temperature to 390⁰F and the timer for 10 minutes.
5. Serve and enjoy.

Nutritional value per serving:

Calories: 462kcal, Carbs: 13g Fat: 28g, Protein: 39g

Crumbled Fish

I love crumbled fish, it's one of my favorite's air-fried meals I am always making in my new instant pot air fryer lid. This crumbled fish is packed with flavor and is without fat.
Prep Time and Cooking Time: 22 minutes| Serves: 4

Ingredients to use:

- 1 cup dry bread crumbs
- 1/4 cup vegetable oil
- 4 eaches flounder fillets
- 1 egg, beaten
- 1 lemon, sliced

Step-by-step Directions to Cook It:

1. Mix bread crumbs and oil in a mixing bowl.
2. Dip the fish fillet in the beaten egg, then in the bread crumbs until well coated.
3. Layer the fillets in the air fryer basket without touching each other. Place the basket in the instant pot.
4. Seal the instant pot with an air fryer lid then set the temperature to 350⁰F and the timer for 12 minutes.
5. Garnish with lemon slices and serve.

Nutritional value per serving:

Calories: 354kcal, Carbs: 22.5g Fat: 17.7g, Protein: 26.9g

Instant pot Air fryer Lid Garlic Shrimp

If you are a shrimp lover, this is a real game-changer. It's a fantastic, easy to cook side dish that every member of your family will love.
Prep Time and Cooking Time: 19 minutes| Serves: 3

Ingredients to use:

- 1 lb. shrimp, peeled and deveined
- Vegetable oil
- 1/4 tbsp. garlic powder
- Salt and pepper to taste

- Lemon wedges
- Parsley, minced

1. Toss shrimp in oil, garlic, salt, and pepper until well coated.
2. Transfer the shrimp in the air fryer basket then place the basket in the instant pot.
3. Seal the instant pot with an air fryer lid. Set temperature to 400^{0}F and the timer for 14 minutes.
4. Transfer the shrimp to a serving platter and squeeze lemon wedges and top with parsley. Enjoy.

Nutritional value per serving:

Calories: 228kcal, Carbs: 1g Fat: 3g, Protein: 46g

Instant pot Air fryer Lid Cod

In less than 20 minutes, this Instant pot air fryer lid cod has the most amazing outer crust and a very tender inside.
Prep Time and Cooking Time: 17 minutes| Serves: 2

Ingredients to use:

- 1 lb. cod fillet
- 1 tbsp. salt
- 1 tbsp. seasoning salt
- 1 lemon, sliced

- 1/4 cup butter

Step-by-step Directions to Cook It:

1. Season the cod fillet with the salt and seasoning salt.
2. Brush the air fryer basket with oil then place the fillet in the basket. Place the basket in the instant pot.
3. Top the cod with lemon slices and butter.
4. Seal the instant pot with an air fryer lid and set the temperature to 400^{0}F and the timer for 13 minutes.
5. The internal temperature should be 145^{0}F when fully cooked, otherwise, cook for more minutes.

Nutritional value per serving:

Calories: 405kcal, Carbs: 5g Fat: 25g, Protein: 41g

Instant pot Air fryer Lid salt and pepper shrimp

Instant pot Air fryer Lid salt and pepper shrimp are far much healthier compared to the deep-fried shrimp. the rice flour gives the shrimp the crunch and makes them gluten-free.
Prep Time and Cooking Time: 20 minutes| Serves: 4

Ingredients to use:

- 2 tbsp. black peppercorns,

ground
- 2 tbsp. Sichuan peppercorns, ground
- 1 tbsp. salt
- 1 tbsp. sugar
- 1 lb. shrimp
- 3 tbsp. rice flour
- 2 tbsp. oil

Step-by-step Directions to Cook It:

1. Set your instant pot to sauté function.
2. Roast the peppercorns for 2 minutes or until you can smell the aroma. Transfer to a bowl and let cool.
3. Wash the inner pot and dry it.
4. Add salt and sugar to the peppercorns and crush using a pestle to form a coarse powder.
5. Place the shrimp in a mixing bowl and add the spices, rice flour, and oil. Mix until the shrimp is well coated.
6. Place the shrimp in an air fryer basket and place the basket in the instant pot. Spray the shrimp with oil.
7. Close the instant pot with an air fryer lid and set temperature 325⁰F and timer for 10 minutes. Toss when halfway cooked.
8. Serve and enjoy.

Nutritional value per serving:

Calories: 178kcal, Carbs: 19g Fat: 8g, Protein: 16g

Popcorn Shrimp

If you are a lover of popcorn shrimp, you don't have to order them in the store anymore. Make your own popcorn shrimp at home in your Instant Pot Duo Crisp Air fryer lid. Prep Time and Cooking Time: 23 minutes| Serves: 6

Ingredients to use:

- 2 eggs, beaten
- 1/4 cup flour
- 1 lb. shrimp, peeled and deveined
- Oil

Coating

- 1 cup bread crumbs
- 1 tbsp. ground cumin
- 1 tbsp. salt
- 1/2 tbsp. pepper
- 1 tbsp. garlic powder

Step-by-step Directions to Cook It:

1. Mix all the coating ingredients and set aside.
2. In a separate bowl, add eggs with 1 tablespoon of water. Pour flour in a plastic bag.
3. Place shrimp in the bag and toss in the flour, then place it in the egg.
4. Pour the breadcrumbs mixture in another plastic bag. Remove the shrimp from the egg and place it in the bag with breadcrumbs.
5. Line the air fryer basket with foil

and spray it with oil. Place the shrimps in the basket and place the basket in the instant pot.

6. Spritz more oil on the shrimp and cover the instant pot with an air fryer lid.

7. Set temperature to 325⁰F and the timer for 8 minutes. Turn the shrimps when halfway cooked

Nutritional value per serving:

Calories: 235kcal, Carbs: 18g Fat: 1g, Protein: 21g

Catfish Fish Fry

There is nothing like a catfish fish fry on a game day, a day out, or on a Friday night. The fish comes out crispy and above all healthy
Prep Time and Cooking Time: 10 minutes| Serves: 2

Ingredients to use:

- 6 catfish fillets
- 1 cup cornmeal
- 1 cup all-purpose flour
- 1 tbsp. old bay
- 1/4 tbsp. paprika
- 1/2 tbsp. kosher salt
- 1/4 tbsp. pepper
- 3/4 cup buttermilk, low-fat

Step-by-step Directions to Cook It:

1. In a mixing bowl, mix cornmeal, flour, old bay, paprika, salt, and pepper.

2. Place buttermilk in a separate bowl. Dip the fish in the flour mixture then in the buttermilk.

3. Place the fish fillet in the air fryer basket and place the basket in the instant pot.

4. Seal the instant pot with an air fryer lid and select air fry. Set temperature to 400⁰F and the timer for 12 minutes.

5. Serve the fish with lemon slices and tartar sauce.

Nutritional value per serving:

Calories: 199kcal, Carbs: 7g Fat: 11.6g, Protein: 15.7g

Stuffed Calamari Mix

A rich cream sauce before serving, this stuffed calamari mix is probably the best calamari you'll ever have.
Prep time and Cooking Time: 35 Minutes | Servings: 4

Ingredients To Use:

- 4 big calamari (tentacles separated and chopped and tubes reserved)
- 2 tablespoon of Parsley (chopped)
- 5 ounces of Kale (chopped)
- 2 garlic cloves (minced)
- 1 red bell pepper (chopped)
- 1 tablespoon of olive oil
- 2 ounces of canned tomato puree
- 1 yellow onion (chopped)
- Salt and black pepper to taste

1. Heat up a pan containing oil over medium heat, and add onion and garlic.
2. Stir gently and cook for about 2 minutes.
3. Add bell pepper, tomato puree, calamari tentacles, kale, salt and pepper, stir gently.
4. Cook for about 10 minutes and remove the heat.
5. Stir gently and cook for 3 minutes.
6. Stuffed calamari tubes in the mix.
7. Hold firmly with toothpicks, then put in your air fryer
8. Cook at a temperature of 360 degrees F for 20 minutes.
9. Divide the calamari on different plates
10. Sprinkle parsley all over and serve.

Nutritional value per serving:

Calories: 110; Fat: 5; Carbs: 15; Protein: 18

Crusted Salmon Mix

Mixed with lemon juice, honey, dill, salt and black pepper. You can make crusted salmon that tastes like it's from a fine seafood restaurant!
Prep time and Cooking Time: 20 Minutes | Servings: 4

Ingredients To Use:

- 1 cup Pistachios (chopped)
- 4 fresh salmon fillets
- 1/4 cup lemon juice
- 1 tsp. Dill (chopped)
- 2 tbsps. honey
- Salt and black pepper to taste
- 1 tbsp. mustard

Step-by-Step Directions to cook it:

1. In a bowl, add pistachios lemon juice, mustard, salt, honey, dill, and black pepper. Whisk well.
2. Spread the pistachios mixture over salmon fillets.
3. Set in your air fryer to cook for 10 mins 350 degrees F.
4. Divide among plates and enjoy alongside a side salad.

Nutritional value per serving:

Calories: 260; Fat: 5; Carbs: 5; Protein: 30

Salmon and Avocado Sauce Mix using Air Fryer

Served with a thick, cool, and creamy avocado lime sauce. Spice up your dinner with salmon and avocado sauce mix using air fryer.
Prep time and Cook Time: 20 Minutes | Servings: 4

Ingredients To Use:

- 1 Avocado (pitted, peeled and

chopped)

- 4 salmon fillets (boneless)
- 1/4 cup Cilantro (chopped)
- 1/3 cup coconut milk
- 1 tbsp. lime juice
- 1 tbsp. lime zest (grated)
- 1 tsp. onion powder
- 1 tsp. garlic powder
- Salt and black pepper to the taste

Step-by-Step Directions to cook it:

1. Season salmon fillets with salt, black pepper and lime zest, rub well.
2. Place inside the air fryer, cook at 350 degrees F for 9 minutes, flipping once.
3. Then divide into different plates
4. Mix the avocado with cilantro, garlic powder, onion powder, lime juice, salt, pepper and coconut milk in a different bowl.
5. Blend properly, and drizzle over salmon
6. Serve immediately.

Nutritional value per serving:

Calories: 240; Fat: 5; Carbs: 11; Protein: 14

Salmon and Orange Marmalade with Side Salad

Easy, quick, few ingredients, delicious, and above all, HEALTHY! In less than thirty minutes, you can serve this wonderful salmon and orange marmalade with side salad. Prep time and Cooking Time: 25 Minutes | Servings: 4

Ingredients To Use:

- 1 pound of wild salmon (skinless, boneless and cubed)
- 2 lemons (sliced)
- 1/4 cup of balsamic vinegar
- 1/4 cup of orange juice
- 1/3 cup of orange marmalade
- A pinch of salt
- black pepper

Step-by-Step Directions to cook it:

1. Heat up a pot containing vinegar over medium-high heat.
2. Then add marmalade as well as orange juice.
3. Stir gently, and bring to a simmer.
4. Cook for about a minute and remove the heat.
5. Thread salmon cubes and lemon slices on skewers, season with salt and black pepper to taste.
6. Brush them with half of the orange marmalade mix.
7. Place neatly in your air fryer's basket; then cook at 360 degrees F for about 3 minutes on each side.
8. Brush skewers with the remaining vinegar mix.
9. Divide into different plates
10. Serve immediately with a side salad

11. Enjoy!

Nutritional value per serving:

calories 240, fat 9g, carbs 14g, protein 10 g

Shrimp and Cauliflower Mix

An easy and delicious cauliflower rice that has low carb and rich in protein recipe!
Prep time and Cooking Time: 22 Minutes | Servings: 2

Ingredients To Use:

- 1 tablespoon of butter
- cooking spray
- 1 riced cauliflower head
- 1 pound of shrimp (peeled and deveined)
- 1/4 cup of heavy cream
- 8 ounces of mushrooms (roughly chopped)
- a pinch of red pepper flakes
- salt and black pepper to taste
- 2 garlic cloves (minced)
- 4 bacon (slices, cooked and crumbled)
- 1/2 cup of beef stock
- 1 tablespoon of parsley (finely chopped)
- 1 tablespoon of chives (chopped)

Step-by-Step Directions to cook it:

1. Season shrimp with salt and pepper, spray with cooking oil, place in your air fryer and cook at 360 degrees F for 7 minutes.
2. Meanwhile, heat up a pan with butter over medium heat, add mushrooms, stir and cook for 3-4 minutes.
3. Add garlic, cauliflower rice, pepper flakes, stock, cream, chives, and parsley.
4. Sprinkle salt and pepper to taste.
5. Stir gently, and cook for some minutes before turning off the heat.
6. Divide the shrimp on different plates.
7. Then add cauliflower mix on the side.
8. Sprinkle bacon as topping
9. Serve immediately.

Nutritional value per serving:

calories 240, fat 9g, carbs 14g, protein 10g

Hot and Creamy Salmon

Dill's bright flavor is perfect for this creamy sauce. Mixed with cheese, mustard and coconut cream.
Prep time and Cooking Time: 20 Minutes | Servings: 4

Ingredients To Use:

- 4 salmon fillets (boneless)
- 1 tablespoon of olive oil
- Salt and black pepper to taste
- 1/3 cup of cheddar cheese (grated)
- 1 and 1/2 teaspoon of mustard

- 1/2 cup of coconut cream

1. Season salmon with salt and pepper, drizzle the oil and rub well.
2. Mix coconut cream with cheddar, mustard, salt and pepper in a bowl and stir well.
3. Transfer salmon to a pan that fits your air fryer, add coconut cream mix, introduce in your air fryer and cook at a temperature of 320 degrees F for about 10 minutes.
4. Divide into different plates
5. Serve immediately.
6. Enjoy!

Nutritional value per serving:

Calories: 240; Fat: 3g; Carbs: 12g; Protein: 20 g

Baked Shrimp Scampi

The fanciest and the easiest dish of all. A tender shrimp with buttery breadcrumbs, garlic and lemon juice.
Prep time and cooking time: 10 minutes | Serves: 4

Ingredients To Use:

- Large shrimp – 1 lb.
- Butter – 8 tbsps.
- Minced garlic – 1 tbsp.
- White wine –1/4 cup
- Salt – 1/2 tsp.
- Cayenne pepper –1/4 tsp.

- Paprika –1/4 tsp.
- Onion powder – 1/2 tsp.
- Bread crumbs – 3/4 cup

Step-by-Step Directions to cook it:

1. Mix bread crumbs with dry seasonings in a bowl.
2. Melt the butter on Sauté with garlic and white wine.
3. Remove from the heat and add the shrimp and bread crumb mix.
4. Transfer this mix to a casserole dish.
5. Choose the Bake option and add food to the air fryer.
6. Cook at 350F for 10 minutes.
7. Serve.

Nutritional value per serving:

Calories 422; Fat 26g; Carbs 18g; Protein 29g

Marinated Salmon

Mixed with oil, garlic and herbs. This marinated salmon is fresh and flavorful. Grilled or baked to perfection.
Prep time and cooking time: 12 minutes | Serves: 4

Ingredients To Use:

- Salmon – 4 fillets
- Brown sugar – 1 tbsp.
- Minced garlic – 1/2 tbsp.
- Soy sauce – 6 tbsps.
- Dijon mustard –1/4 cup

- Chopped green onion – 1

1. In a bowl, mix mustard, soy sauce, brown sugar, and minced garlic.
2. Pour this mixture over salmon fillets and coat well.
3. Marinate for 30 minutes in the refrigerator.
4. Then cook in the air fryer at 400F for 12 minutes.
5. Garnish with green onions and serve.

Nutritional value per serving:

Calories 267; Fat 11g; Carbs 5g; Protein 37g

Air Fryer Fish

It is every bit as crunchy and the fish stays perfectly flaky. This air fryer fish is absolutely flavorful and delicious.

Prep time and cooking time: 17 minutes | Serves: 4

Ingredients To Use:

- Whitefish fillets - 4
- Cooking spray
- Fish seasoning
- Very fine cornmeal – 3/4 cup
- Flour –1/4 cup
- Old bay seasoning – 2 tsps.
- Salt – 1-1/2 tsps.
- Paprika – 1 tsp.
- Garlic powder –1/2 tsp.

- Black pepper –1/2 tsp.

Step-by-Step Directions to cook it:

1. Put the ingredients for fish seasoning in a Ziplock bag and shake well.
2. Set aside.
3. Place the fish fillets in the Ziplock bag and shake well to coat.
4. Grease the air fryer basket with cooking spray.
5. Cook the fillets for 10 minutes at 400F.
6. Open and spray the fish with oil.
7. Then flip and cook for 7 minutes more.
8. Serve.

Nutritional value per serving:

Calories 193; Fat 1g; Carbs 27g; Protein 19g

Lobster Tails

High end type and most elegant lobster that usually reserved for a special occasions at pricey restaurants. Mixed with lemon juice, garlic, butter and salt for better taste.

Prep time and cooking time: 8 minutes | Serves: 8

Ingredients To Use:

- Lobster tails – 2 (6 oz.) butterflied
- Salt – 1 tsp.
- Chopped chives – 1 tsp.

- Unsalted butter – 2 tbsps. melted
- Minced garlic -1 tbsp.
- Lemon juice – 1 tsp.

Step-by-Step Directions to cook it:

1. Combine garlic, butter, salt, chives, and lemon juice.
2. Spread the lobster tails with butter mix and cook in the air fryer at 380F for 4 minutes. Then open and spread more butter on top.
3. Cook for 2 to 4 minutes more.
4. Serve.

Nutritional value per serving:

Calories 120; Fat 12g; Carbs 2g; Protein 1g

Chapter 6: Soups, Stews, and Broths

Creamy Chicken Stew

This stew is all shades of amazing. It is healthy, creamy, and delicious. You can eat this stew alone or as a side dish.

Prep time and cooking time: 35 minutes | Serves: 4

Ingredients To Use:

- 1-1/2 cup of canned cream of celery soup
- 6 chicken tenders
- Salt and black pepper, as desired
- 2 potatoes, chopped
- 1 bay leaf
- 1 thyme spring, chopped
- 1 Tbsp. milk
- 1 egg yolk
- 1/2 cup of heavy cream

Step-by-Step Directions to Cook It:

1. Mix the chicken, potatoes, cream of celery, thyme, bay leaf, salt, and black pepper. Toss until the chicken is well coated, then transfer to the basket of the air fryer.
2. Cover the air fryer with the Instant Pot Duo Crisp Air Fryer Lid and select the Air Fry Smart Program.
3. Set the timer to 25 minutes and 320°F.
4. Allow the stew to cool for a few minutes, then discard the bay leaf and serve into plates.

Nutritional value per serving:

Calories: 300kcal, Fat: 11g, Carbs: 23g, Protein: 14g

Chicken Consommé

The egg white and eggshells used in this recipe is to make the soup sparkling clear. This is a shortcut recipe for a delicious meal.

Prep time and cooking time: 50 minutes | Serves: 4

Ingredients To Use:

- 6 cup of canned chicken broth
- 3 large egg, whites separated and whisked, shells reserved
- 3 scallions with tops, sliced
- 1 tomato, sliced
- 1 small carrot, sliced
- 1/2 cup of chopped fresh parsley
- 1/2 tsp. of dried thyme
- 1/2 tsp. of dried basil
- 6 whole black peppercorns

- 1 bay leaf

Step-by-Step Directions to
Cook It:

1. Mix the broth, egg whites, shells,
   scallions, carrot, tomato, parsley,
   basil, thyme, bay leaf, and
   peppercorns. Transfer the
   mixture to the Instant Pot cooker
   base and cover with the Instant
   Pot Duo Crisp Air Fryer Lid.
2. Select the Broil Smart Program
   and set the timer to 36 minutes
   at 370°F.
3. Sieve the soup through a fine-
   mesh into a heatproof dish.
   Discard the solids accumulated
   in the mesh, skim off the fat on
   the soup and serve into bowls.

Nutritional value per serving:

Calories: 130kcal, Fat: 13g, Carbs: 18g,
Protein: 9g

Tofu Vegetable Soup

This deliciously light soup is packed
with vitamin C and protein. It can be
prepared in less than 20 minutes.
Prep time and cooking time: 15
minutes | Serves: 4

Ingredients To Use:

- 1-1/2 cup of chicken stock
- 2 Tbsp. rice vinegar
- 6 scallions, sliced
- 2 Tbsp. ketchup
- 1 Tbsp. sesame oil

- 3/4 tsp. salt
- 1 pound of firm tofu, divided into
  1-inch chunks
- 3 cup of shredded Napa cabbage
- 2 carrots, sliced
- 1/2 tsp. ground ginger

Step-by-Step Directions to
Cook It:

1. To the Instant Pot cooker base,
   add the water, chicken stock,
   ketchup, vinegar, salt, oil, and
   ginger.
2. Stir and cover with the
   broil/dehydration tray and the
   Instant Pot Duo Crisp Air Fryer
   Lid. Set the timer to 10 minutes
   at 360°F.
3. After 5 minutes, carefully remove
   the cover of the instant pot and
   add the tofu, carrots, cabbage,
   and scallions. Leave to cook for
   the rest of the cooking time.
4. Divide into equal portions and
   serve.

Nutritional value per serving:

Calories: 154kcal, Fat: 7g, Carbs: 9g,
Protein: 14g

Greek Egg and Lemon Soup

This is a classic Greek soup that can
serve as a first course for lunch and
dinner.
Prep time and cooking time: 50
minutes | Serves: 6

- 1 Tbsp. olive oil
- 1 yellow onion, thinly sliced
- 6 lemon slices
- 8 cups of homemade chicken stock
- 2 eggs, whisked
- 1/3 cup of lemon juice
- 1-1/2 tsp. salt
- Snipped dill sprigs
- 1/4 cup of fresh dill

Step-by-Step Directions to Cook It:

1. Set the empty cooker base to Sauté mode and heat the oil. Stir in the oil and fry for 3 minutes.
2. Add the chicken stock, and cover with the Instant Pot Duo Crisp Air Fryer Lid. Select the Broil Smart Program and set the timer to 20 minutes at 300°F.
3. After 20 minutes, add the eggs, lemon juice, and salt. Replace the Instant Pot Duo Crisp Air Fryer Lid and select the Broil Smart Program at 250°F for 3 minutes.
4. Serve.

Nutritional value per serving:

Calories: 98kcal, Fat: 4g, Carbs: 8g, Protein: 2g

Chive Vichyssoise

Here is a chilled potato soup that is sure to improve the flavor of your entire meal. Buttermilk, rather than heavy cream, is used to reduce the calorie content.

Prep time and cooking time: 30 minutes | Serves: 4

Ingredients To Use:

- 1 Tbsp. unsalted butter
- 2 tsp. of lemon juice
- 1 medium yellow onion, sliced
- 1 medium leek, sliced
- 1/4 tsp. of hot red pepper sauce
- 1 medium celery stalk, sliced
- 2 medium potatoes, peeled and cubed
- 1 3/4 cup of chicken broth
- 1 cup of buttermilk
- 1 Tbsp. minced fresh chives

Step-by-Step Directions to Cook It:

1. Set the empty cooker base to Sauté mode and melt the butter. Stir in the onions, celery, and leek. Sauté for 3 minutes.
2. Add the broth, set the broil/dehydration tray, and cover with the Instant Pot Duo Crisp Air Fryer Lid.
3. Set the timer to 20 minutes at 350°F.
4. Transfer the soup to a food processor and blend for 30 seconds. Add the chives, lemon juice, buttermilk, pepper sauce, and lemon juice.
5. Transfer the blended mixture to a bowl and keep in the refrigerator for 3 hours.

6. Serve.

Nutritional value per serving:

Calories: 121kcal, Fat: 9g, Carbs: 15g, Protein: 8g

White Borscht

White Borscht is a popular European recipe that is cooked with potatoes rather than beets. It is delicious and easy.

Prep time and cooking time: 30 minutes | Serves: 4

Ingredients To Use:

- 3/4 pound of red potatoes, thinly sliced
- 3 cups of buttermilk
- 1 large cucumber, thinly sliced
- 1 small red onion, thinly sliced
- 1/3 cup of walnuts
- 3/4 tsp. salt
- 3 chicken sausages, sliced
- 1/2 tsp. black pepper
- 3/4 cup of thinly sliced radishes, cut thinly
- 1/4 cup of snipped fresh dill

Step-by-Step Directions to Cook It:

1. Add the potatoes to the Instant Pot cooker base, add water to cover, then seal with the Instant Pot Duo Crisp Air Fryer Lid.
2. Select the Smart Broil program and set the timer for 10 minutes at 350°F.

3. Remove the cooked potatoes, drain, and set aside
4. Add the cucumber, walnuts, onion, salt, pepper, and 2 cups of buttermilk to a food processor and pulse until a smooth mixture is obtained.
5. Serve the walnut mixture into bowls, stir in the leftover buttermilk, reserved potatoes, dill, and radishes.
6. Cover the bowls and keep refrigerated for 3 hours.
7. Serve cold.

Nutritional value per serving:

Calories: 145kcal, Fat: 14g, Carbs: 19g, Protein: 8g

Chunky Seafood Chowder

This seafood chowder recipe is the complete package. It is rich with crab, soft potatoes, onions, and clams.
Prep time and cooking time: 35 minutes| Serves: 8

Ingredients To Use:

- 2 Tbsp. butter
- 1 medium onion, chopped
- 2 pints of half-and-half
- 1 can of New England clam chowder
- 3 medium potatoes, diced
- 1 tsp. salt
- 1/4 tsp. white pepper
- 8 ounces of crabmeat, flaked

1. Set the empty cooker base to Sauté mode and melt the butter. Stir in the onion and fry for about 2 minutes.
2. Add the clam chowder, half and half, potatoes, salt, and black pepper. Cover with the broil/dehydration tray and the Instant Pot Duo Crisp Air Fryer Lid.
3. Select the Broil Smart Program and set the timer for 15 minutes at 370°F.
4. When ready, add the crab meat and cook for another 8 minutes at the same temperature.

Nutritional value per serving:

Calories: 189kcal, Fat: 13g, Carbs: 23g, Protein: 11g

Gingered Tofu and Noodle Soup

The ginger and scallions used in this recipe add a spark to this otherwise delicate soup.
Prep time and cooking time: 30 minutes | Serves: 4

Ingredients To Use:

- 8 ounces of fine egg noodles, cooked
- 2 Tbsp. olive oil
- 5 scallions, sliced into 1-inch slices
- 3 Tbsp. minced fresh ginger
- 5 cups of chicken stock
- 1 small head cabbage, thinly sliced
- 12 ounces of firm tofu, chopped into 1/2-inch cubes
- 1/4 tsp. salt
- 1/8 tsp. of black pepper

Step-by-Step Directions to Cook It:

1. Toss the cooked noodles with 1 tbsp. of olive oil.
2. Set the empty cooker base to Sauté mode and heat the oil. Stir in the ginger and scallions—Fry for about 2 minutes.
3. Add the stock and cabbage, then cover with the broil/dehydration tray and the Instant Pot Duo Crisp Air Fryer Lid.
4. Select the Broil Smart Program and set the timer for 10 minutes at 350°F.
5. Stir in the tofu, noodles, and season with salt and black pepper.
6. Allow cooling for 2 minutes before serving.

Nutritional value per serving:

Calories: 136kcal, Fat: 12g, Carbs: 17g, Protein: 8g

Minestrone

The beauty of a Minestrone is that everything goes as long as it's a hearty mixture of vegetables, pasta, rice, or white beans. For vegetarians, the beef stock can be substituted with vegetable broth.

Prep time and cooking time: 50 minutes | Serves: 6

Ingredients To Use:

- 1 Tbsp. olive oil
- 1 large yellow onion, chopped
- 2 garlic cloves, grated
- 3-1/2 cup of beef broth
- 15 ounces of great Northern beans, rinsed and drained
- 1-3/4 cup of chopped tomatoes, cut up and left undrained
- 2 cups of roughly shredded cabbage
- 2 large carrots, thinly chopped
- 1 tsp. dried oregano
- 1 tsp. dried basil
- 1/2 tsp. salt
- 1/2 tsp. black pepper
- 2 ounces of vermicelli, broken
- 1 small zucchini, and sliced
- Shredded Parmesan cheese

Step-by-Step Directions to Cook It:

1. Set the empty cooker base to Sauté mode and heat the oil. Stir in the garlic and onion—Fry for about 3 minutes.

2. Add the broth, tomatoes, beans, cabbage, oregano, carrots, basil, salt, and black pepper.
3. Cover with the broil/dehydration tray and the Instant Pot Duo Crisp Air Fryer Lid. Select the Broil Smart Program and set the timer for 5 minutes at 350°F.
4. Add the vermicelli and replace the cover.
5. Increase the timer of the Instant Pot Duo Crisp Air Fryer Lid to 15 minutes. Maintain the same temperature.
6. Add the zucchini, cook for another 33 minutes, then transfer the contents to plates.
7. Serve with grated cheese.

Nutritional value per serving:

Calories: 259kcal, Fat: 26g, Carbs: 31g, Protein: 8g

Hot, Hot Chili Soup

This recipe is for the lovers of spicy soup. It is dangerously hot and spicy and is not for the meek. If you love a good spicy meal, challenge yourself with this recipe.

Prep time and cooking time: 2 hours 10 minutes | Serves: 8

Ingredients To Use:

- 2 Tbsp. vegetable oil
- 2 pounds of beef stew meat, cut into pieces
- 1 medium onion, thinly sliced

- 3 garlic cloves, grated
- 16 ounces of hot banana peppers, chopped
- 29 ounces of diced tomatoes, left undrained
- 10 ounces of diced tomatoes and green chiles, left undrained
- 6 ounces of tomato paste
- 16 ounces of kidney beans, rinsed and drained
- 4 ounces of chopped green chiles
- 1 fresh jalapeno pepper, seeded and chopped
- 2 Tbsp. chili powder
- 1-1/2 Tbsp. hot red pepper sauce
- 1 tsp. salt
- 1/8 tsp. ground cumin
- Whole banana peppers

Step-by-Step Directions to Cook It:

1. Set the empty cooker base to Sauté mode and heat the oil. Stir in the garlic, beef, and onion. Fry for about 5 minutes until meat is browned.
2. Add the chopped hot peppers, diced tomatoes, tomato paste, tomato and chiles, chili powder, jalapeno pepper, cumin, red pepper sauce, and sauce.
3. Cover with the broil/dehydration tray and the Instant Pot Duo Crisp Air Fryer Lid. Select the Broil Smart Program and set the timer for 2 hours at 300°F.

4. Garnish with whole banana peppers and serve.

Nutritional value per serving:

Calories: 131kcal, Fat: 6g, Carbs: 12g, Protein: 8g

Instant pot Lentil soup

This is a delicious, quick to make soup simply made in the instant pot. It's packed with vegetables and is perfect for any time of the year
Prep Time and Cooking Time: 23 minutes| Serves: 2

Ingredients to use:

- 2-1/2 cups vegetable stock
- 1-1/4 cups lentils, dried
- 1-1/2 cups butternut squash, cubed
- 4 carrots, diced
- 4 celery stalks, diced
- 1 onion, quartered
- 15 oz. fire roast tomatoes
- Salt and pepper
- Lacinato kale

Step-by-step Directions to Cook It:

1. Add the vegetable stock, lentils, butternut squash, carrots, celery, and onion in the inner pot of your instant pot. Stir well.
2. Dump the tomatoes on top of everything.
3. Seal the lid and press the soup button. Adjust time for 8 minutes.
4. Release pressure quickly then

add kale and stir.
5. Season with salt and pepper.
6. Serve with crusty bread and enjoy.

Nutritional value per serving:

Calories: 342kcal, Carbs: 84g Fat: -g, Protein: 25g

Instant pot Chicken Taco Soup

This is a hearty taco soup that is made in the instant pot with hardly any effort. It's topped with creamy avocado and melty cheese making it an all-time soup.
Prep Time and Cooking Time: 40 minutes| Serves: 6

Ingredients to use:

- 2 chicken breasts, boneless and skinless
- 1 onion, diced
- 15 oz. can chicken broth
- 15 oz. can kidney beans
- 15 oz. can corn
- 15 oz. tomatoes, diced
- 8 oz. can tomato sauce
- 2 tbsp. taco seasoning
- 2 tbsp. Dry ranching seasoning,
- sour cream, cheese, tomatoes and avocado for garnish

Step-by-step Directions to Cook It:

1. Place the chicken in the instant pot.

2. Top with all other ingredients except for the garnish.
3. Seal the instant pot list and select the soup function. Set timer for 30 minutes.
4. Release pressure quickly. Remove the soup and shred the chicken into bite-size pieces.
5. Serve the soup garnished to your liking.

Nutritional value per serving:

Calories: 52kcal, Carbs: 2g Fat: -g, Protein: 8g

Rotisserie chicken soup

This is a perfect winter soup that is quick and easy to make in the instant pot. You will love the soup as well as every member of your family.
Prep Time and Cooking Time: 35 minutes| Serves: 4

Ingredients to use:

- 1 chicken rotisserie
- 64 oz. chicken stock, low sodium
- 2 cup zucchini, diced
- 1 cup carrots, diced
- 1 tbsp. pepper
- 1/2 cup brown rice, dry
- 1-1/2 cup salsa

Step-by-step Directions to Cook It:

1. Chop the chicken into bite-size pieces. Cop the bones and skin as the same size as the meat
2. Add the chicken with other

ingredients in the instant pot.

3. Close the lid and cook on high pressure using the soup setting for 25 minutes.
4. Release pressure naturally, and then remove the bones and skin.
5. Garnish the soup with cilantro, avocado or tortilla strips

Nutritional value per serving:

Calories: 568kcal, Carbs: 24g Fat: 32g, Protein: 48g

Instant pot Vegetable Soup

This instant pot vegetable soup is perfect for people who don't love vegetables but love soup. It's a great way of serving veggies in their meals.
Prep Time and Cooking Time: 17 minutes| Serves: 8

Ingredients to use:

- 1 tbsp. canola oil
- 1 onion, diced
- 2 tbsp. garlic, minced
- 2 tbsp. Italian seasoning
- 2 tbsp. salt
- 1/4 tbsp. black pepper
- 6 cups chicken broth, low sodium
- 1 lb. potatoes, chopped
- 3 carrots, peeled and chopped
- 2 ribs celery, sliced
- 1 cup green beans, fresh and cut in thirds
- 1-1/2 cups chopped tomatoes, fire-roasted
- 1 cup spinach, finely chopped

Step-by-step Directions to Cook It:

1. Set the instant pot to sauté mode. Sauté onions in oil until soft. Turn it off.
2. Add garlic, seasoning, salt, and pepper and cook in the residual heat for 1 minute.
3. Add broth and scrape the bottom with a spoon.
4. Add all other ingredients except for the spinach and close the lid.
5. Cook for 2 minutes then release the pressure manually for 10 minutes.
6. Open the lid and stir in spinach. Serve.

Nutritional value per serving:

Calories: 101kcal, Carbs: 17g Fat: 1g, Protein: 6g

Instant pot Potato Soup

This will be your favorite potato soup. Its ultimately comforting, creamy, and loaded with potatoes plus other veggies.
Prep Time and Cooking Time: 35 minutes| Serves: 6

Ingredients to use:

- 2 lb. red potatoes, sliced
- 3 cups chicken broth
- 2 carrots, peeled and sliced
- 1 rib celery, chopped
- 1-1/2 tbsp. salt
- 1 tbsp. garlic, minced

- 1 tbsp. parsley, dried
- 1/2 tbsp. thyme, dried
- 1 tbsp. onion powder
- A pinch black pepper
- 1 cup evaporated milk
- 2 tbsp. corn starch
- Green onions, cheese, and bacon for garnish.

Step-by-step Directions to Cook It:

1. Add all ingredients except milk and corn starch.
2. Close the lid and set 3 minutes on high pressure. It will take about 20 minutes to build up pressure and cook.
3. Release pressure quickly then set the instant pot to sauté setting.
4. Mix milk and corn starch in a bowl then stir into the soup. Cook until thickened.
5. Season with salt and pepper then garnish to your liking.
6. Serve.

Nutritional value per serving:

Calories: 54kcal, Carbs: 9g Fat: -g, Protein: -g

Instant Pot Beef Stew

This is an ultimately hearty simple mid-week dinner. It's simple, melt in the mouth dish that everyone will love.

Prep Time and Cooking Time: 1 hour

25 minutes| Serves: 4

Ingredients to use:

- 1 tbsp. butter
- 1 lb. beef chuck, cubed
- 4 Yukon Gold potatoes, cubed
- 1-1/2 cup mushrooms, halved
- 1 onion, sliced into wedges
- 2 carrots, sliced
- 2 garlic cloves, minced
- 3 cups beef broth
- 1 tbsp. Worcestershire sauce
- 1 tbsp. tomato paste
- 1 tbsp. salt
- 1/2 tbsp. black pepper
- 1/2 tbsp. rosemary, dried

Step-by-step Directions to Cook It:

1. Set your instant pot to sauté function. Melt butter and cook the beef until browned on all sides. You may cook in batches.
2. Add all other ingredients and stir well to mix. Close the lid and select the stew function.
3. Set the timer for 35 minutes allowing pressure to build in for 15 minutes.
4. Release pressure naturally for 30 minutes.
5. Remove the lid and serve the stew.

Nutritional value per serving:

Calories: 351kcal, Carbs: 32.2g Fat: 16.4g, Protein: 20g

Instant pot hamburger soup

This is a simple Instant pot soup that uses everyday ingredients. It's flavorful, healthy, easy to make comfort food that everyone will love.
Prep Time and Cooking Time: 42 minutes| Serves: 6

Ingredients to use:

- 1/2 tbsp. olive oil
- 1/2 onion, chopped
- 2 sticks celery. Chopped
- 1 lb. ground beef, extra lean
- 3 garlic cloves
- 2 tbsp. tomato paste
- 1 can tomatoes, diced
- 2 Russet potatoes, diced
- 1 dash Italian Seasoning
- Salt and pepper

Step-by-step Directions to Cook It:

1. Press the sauté button on your instant pot. Sauté oil, onions and celery for 4 minutes.
2. Stir in beef and cook until it's browned. Drain any excess fat if you desire.
3. Add all other ingredients and seal the lid. Cook on high pressure for 8 minutes.
4. Quickly release the pressure then season the stew with salt and pepper to taste.
5. Serve and enjoy.

Nutritional value per serving:
Calories: 253kcal, Carbs: 30g Fat: 6g, Protein: 22g

Instant pot summer soup

The instant summer soup is comforting and brings out a fresh filling that makes you want to eat more and more of it.
Prep Time and Cooking Time: 50 minutes| Serves: 2

Ingredients to use:

- 1 lb. chicken breasts
- 28 oz. crushed tomatoes
- 4 carrots, peeled and chopped
- 2 celery stalks, chopped
- 3 garlic cloves, minced
- 1/2 cup farro
- 6 cups chicken broth
- 2 tbsp. olive oil
- 1 tbsp. each basil and oregano
- 1/2 tbsp. onion and garlic powder
- 2 tbsp. salt
- 3 cups sweet corn kernels, fresh
- 2 zucchini, diced
- Toppings: lemon juice, parmesan cheese, yogurt, fresh ground pepper

Step-by-step Directions to Cook It:

1. Add everything in the instant pot except corn and zucchini. Seal the instant pot and cook for 20 minutes on high pressure.
2. Remove the stew from the

instant pot and shred the chicken. Stir in corn and zucchini.
3. Close the lid and cook for 5 more minutes under high pressure. Release pressure and let the stew rest before serving.
4. Add your favorite topping and enjoy.

Calories: 217kcal, Carbs: 24g Fat: 7.2g, Protein: 18.3g

Instant pot Noodle stew

If you are a lover of chicken noodle stew and has always been making it in the old way, then this instant pot version will amaze you.
Prep Time and Cooking Time: 20 minutes| Serves: 6

Ingredients to use:

- 1 onion
- 1 tbsp. olive oil
- 2 chicken breast
- 1 cup carrot, sliced
- 1 cup celery
- 1 tbsp. parsley
- 1 bay leaf
- 6 cups chicken broth
- 4 oz. egg noodles
- Salt and pepper

Step-by-step Directions to Cook It:

1. Set your instant pot to sauté function.
2. Cook onions in oil until soft.

3. Add all ingredients except the noodles and select the soup setting. Cook on high pressure and set time for 10 minutes.
4. Release pressures quickly, remove and discard the bay leaf. Remove chicken breast from the instant pot and shred it using forks.
5. Turn the instant pot to sauté function and add the noodles once the stew begins to boil. Let simmer for 8 minutes or until tender.
6. Return the chickens and season with salt and pepper. Enjoy.

Nutritional value per serving:

Calories: 198kcal, Carbs: 17g Fat: 5g, Protein: 19g

Instant pot minestrone soup

This is the coziest, flavorful, and the best minestrone soup you will ever serve your friends coming over or family.
Prep Time and Cooking Time: 10 minutes| Serves: 2

Ingredients to use:

- 2 tbsp. olive oil
- 3 garlic cloves
- 1 onion, diced
- 2 carrots, peeled and diced
- 2 celery stalks, diced
- 1-1/2 tbsp. oregano, dried

- 1/2 tbsp. fennel seed1/2 tbsp. fennel seed
- 6 cups chicken broth, low sodium
- 28 oz. tomatoes, diced
- 16 oz. kidney beans, drained and rinsed
- 1 zucchini, chopped
- 1 parmesan rind
- 1 bay leaf
- 1 bunch kale, stems and leaves removed
- 2 tbsp. red wine vinegar
- Salt and pepper to taste
- 1/3 cup parmesan cheese, freshly grated
- 2 tbsp. parsley leaves

1. Set the instant pot to the sauté setting.
2. Sauté garlic, onions, carrots, and celery in oil while stirring occasionally for 3 minutes.
3. Add basil, oregano, and feel seed to the instant pot and cook until fragrant.
4. Add other ingredients as they follow up to the bay leaf. Close the lid and set the time for 5 minutes on high pressure.
5. Quick-release pressure and add kale. Stir until wilted. Stir in vinegar and season with salt and pepper.
6. Serve garnished with cheese and parsley. Enjoy.

Nutritional value per serving:

Calories: 227kcal, Carbs: 26g Fat: 7g, Protein: 14g

Instant pot whole chicken Bones Broth

You can easily make this instant pot bone broth in your home using readily available ingredients. The broth can be used in other recipes or as a nourishing beverage.

Prep Time and Cooking Time: 3 hours 5 minutes| Serves: 8

Ingredients to use:
- 1 whole chicken bones
- 1 onion, halved
- 1 head garlic
- 2 ribs of celery
- 2 carrots
- A few sprigs of rosemary and thyme
- 1 bay leaf
- 1 tbsp. black peppercorns
- 1 tbsp. salt
- 1 tbsp. apple cider vinegar
- water

Step-by-step Directions to Cook It:

1. Add all ingredients then cover with water in the instant pot.
2. Close the instant pot lid and set the valve to sealing. Cook for 2 hours on high pressure or for 3 hours on low pressure.

3. Allow pressure to be released naturally for 30 minutes.
4. Place the strainer over a bowl and use a slotted spoon to remove large solids from the instant pot. Pour the rest through the strainer and wait until all liquid has drained.
5. Serve or allow to cool and store up to 5 days in the fridge

Calories: 86kcal, Carbs: -g Fat: 2.9g, Protein: 5g

Instant pot Bone broth

This instant pot bone broth is the easiest to make in the instant pot. Its nutritious, pale, and whole 30. It's perfect for the cold weather season.
Prep Time and Cooking Time: 3 hours 30 minutes| Serves: 12

Ingredients to use:
- 2 lb. bones
- 6 quarts water
- 1 cup celery stalks, halved
- 1 cup carrots, halved
- 1 cup onion, halved

Step-by-step Directions to Cook It:

1. Add all ingredients in the instant pot.
2. Cover the instant pot and set time for 120 minutes on high pressure. Allow the instant pot to release pressure naturally.

3. Let the broth slightly cool then run through a strainer into a bowl.
4. Add the vegetables in a blender and add some broth. Blend until smooth then add into the broth.
5. Stir well and serve. You may also store it in airtight containers for up to 4 days.

Nutritional value per serving:

Calories: 17kcal, Carbs: 4g Fat: 1g, Protein: 1g

Vegetable Broth

Are you tired of buying broth from the store? If yes this is a recipe for you. Its easy, flavorful, and above all pocket friendly.
Prep Time and Cooking Time: 10 minutes| Serves: 2

Ingredients to use:
- 2 yellow onions
- 3 celery stalks
- 4 carrots
- 3 garlic cloves
- 2 bay leaves
- 1 tbsp. peppercorns
- 3 sprigs thyme, fresh
- 1 tbsp. tomato paste
- 1 tbsp. shiitake, dried
- 1 tbsp. kosher salt
- 8 cups cold water

Step-by-step Directions to Cook It:

1. Add all ingredients in the instant pot, cover, and set time for 15

minutes on high pressure.
2. Naturally, release all the pressure.
3. Strain the solids through a strainer into a bowl.
4. Serve the stock or allow to cool then store in airtight containers

Calories: 18kcal, Carbs: 4g Fat: 1g, Protein: 1g

Easy Instant pot vegetable broth

Make this nourishing vegetable stock in your instant pot to serve as is or to add into other recipes to deen the flavors
Prep Time and Cooking Time: 25 minutes| Serves: 2

Ingredients to use:

- 2 small onions
- 2 celery stalks
- 2 carrots, diced
- 2 bay leaves
- 1 shiitake mushroom, dried
- 6 cremini mushrooms, sliced
- 4 garlic cloves, crushed
- 1 tbsp. whole peppercorn
- 2 tbsp. regular soy sauce
- 8 cups water
- Dried herbs

Step-by-step Directions to Cook It:

1. Place all ingredients in an instant pot.

2. Close the lid and set time for 15 minutes on high pressure. Naturally, release pressure for 15 minutes then release the rest of the pressure quickly.
3. Open the lid carefully then strain the vegetable broth through a fine-mesh strainer.
4. Serve or let cool to refrigerate

Calories: 28kcal, Carbs: 6g Fat: 3g, Protein: 3g

Instant pot Umami Vegetable Broth

This instant pot recipe uses umami ingredients which add to the depth of the flavors. Roasting the vegetables first also adds to the complexity of the broth.
Prep Time and Cooking Time: 25 minutes| Serves: 2

Ingredients to use:

- 5 carrots, sliced
- 3 stalks celery, sliced
- 1 onion, sliced
- 1garlic bulb, halved
- 4 cups additional vegetables
- 4" square kombu
- A handful of shiitake mushrooms, dried

Step-by-step Directions to Cook It:

1. Arrange the vegetables in the air

fryer basket except for the greens, kombu, and mushrooms. Place the basket in the instant pot.
2. Seal the instant pot using the air fryer lid and select roast function. Roast until the edges are browned.
3. Transfer the roasted vegetables to the instant pot inner pot and add the rest of the vegetable.
4. Add water and close the instant pot lid. Set time for 30 minutes on high pressure.
5. Let rest for 10 minutes before releasing pressure.
6. Strain the broth through a strainer into serving bowls or into mason jars for storage.

Nutritional value per serving:

Calories: 40kcal, Carbs: 5g Fat: 1g, Protein: 2g

Broccoli and Cheese Soup

This soup is great and very flavorful. Just add one cup of sliced mushrooms or one cup of white wine with onions for better taste.
Prep Time and Cooking Time: 20 minutes | Serves: 4

Ingredients To Use:

- 1 cup heavy cream
- 4 cups of broccoli – florets
- 4 cloves of garlic
- 3-1/2 cups of vegetable broth
- 3 cups cheddar cheese, shredded

Step-by-Step Directions to cook it:

1. Cut the broccoli into florets and mince the garlic. Sauté the garlic over medium heat in a large pot for 1 minute or until garlic is fragrant.
2. Combine the vegetable broth, chopped broccoli, and heavy cream in the pot. Boil first and then decrease to simmer for 10 - 20 minutes. Check that the vegetables are soft.
3. Remove about 1/3 broccoli and set aside.
4. Then insert the immersion blender into the pot and puree all the ingredients together.
5. Reduce the heat and add the shredded cheddar cheese about 1/2 cup at a time. Repeatedly swirl until the cheese is melted. Then puree the soup again to make a smooth consistency.
6. Remove from heat and garnish with remaining broccoli florets.

Nutrition Facts Per Serving:

Calories 292, Fat 45 g, Carbs 8 g, Protein 60 g

Zucchini Soup

A delicious soup served anytime. Mixed with heavy cream, chicken broth, onion, garlic and salt and pepper.

Prep Time and Cooking Time: 30 minutes | Serves: 4

Ingredients To Use:

- 1/4 cup heavy cream
- 16 oz. chicken broth
- 7 oz. onion, sliced
- 2 cloves garlic
- 28 oz. zucchini, sliced
- Pepper and salt as desired

Step-by-Step Directions to cook it:

1. Pre-cut the zucchini and onion into slices.
2. Add sliced onion and zucchini, garlic and broth to a large pot. Boil and then decrease to moderate heat and let the soup simmer for about 20 minutes. Keep stirring.
3. Remove pot from heat once the zucchini is soft and insert an immersion blender to puree the soup.
4. Keep blending until smooth. Add in heavy cream, salt, and pepper and stir thoroughly.

Nutrition Facts Per Serving:

Calories 292, Fat 45 g, Carbs 8 g, Protein 60 g

Burly Beef Stew

These burly beef stew is good on chilly nights. A classic stew with mushrooms and potatoes, carrots and tender beef.

Prep time and cooking time: 105 minutes | Serves: 8

Ingredients To Use:

- 2 tablespoons of clarified butter or ghee
- 2 pounds of stew beef (cut it into bite-sized pieces)
- 1 chopped onion
- 1 quart of beef broth
- 1 16-ounce can of cremini mushrooms

Step-by-Step Directions to cook it:

1. Start with the sauté option on your pressure cooker and start melting the butter in it. Brown the meat for 2-3 minutes, making sure it's seared on all sides. (Work in smaller batches to prevent overcrowding the pot.) Take each batch out, put it on a plate and set aside.
2. Into the pot, add the onion, sprinkle it with a bit of salt and let it sauté. The liquid it releases will help you deglaze the pot of any browned bits.
3. When the onions are caramelized, add the beef back into the pot along with the rest of the ingredients. Close the lid and the valve. Use the meat/stew option or the pressure cook function and set the timer for 35 minutes.
4. After the time is up, let the pressure release on its own

(should take 30-35 minutes). Remove the lid – if it seems like there's too much liquid, simply ladle out a bit.

5. Serve in warm bowls with a little parsley garnish.

Calories 411, Fat 27 g, Carbs 11 g, Protein 26 g

Broth Cheddar Soup

This creamy cheese soup is delicious on a cold winter day! You can serve this in less than twenty minutes.
Prep time and cooking time: 15 minutes | Serves: 8

Ingredients To Use:

- 1 diced onion
- 2 small heads of broccoli, chopped
- 4 cups of chicken broth
- 1 12-ounce can of evaporated milk
- 8 ounces of grated sharp cheddar

Step-by-Step Directions to cook it:

1. Start by sautéing the onion in a little bit of olive oil. Stir frequently and cook for 5-6 minutes.
2. Once the onions are cooked, add in the chicken broth and broccoli. Mix it thoroughly and close the lid and valve. Cook under high pressure for 5-6 minutes.

3. After the time is up, release the pressure and open the lid. Switch the pot to simmer setting and pour in the evaporated milk.
4. Gently stir continuously and slowly sprinkle in cheese by a handful. Don't rush, make sure the previous batch of cheese is melted before adding the next and keep adding until you run out of cheese. Taste for seasoning, add salt and pepper as needed.
5. Ladle the soup into warm bowls and serve with herbal garnish.

Nutritional value per serving:

Calories: 426.2, Fat: 34.8 g, Carbs: 12.4 g, Protein: 17.7 g

Tingly Tomato Soup

Rich with flavor and texture. This tingly tomato soup is easy to make and super delicious.
Prep time and cooking time: 8 minutes | Serves: 8

Ingredients To Use:

- 2 tablespoons of olive oil
- 1 small white onion, chopped
- 28 ounces of canned fire-roasted tomatoes
- 3/4 of a cup of vegetable broth
- 2 teaspoons of dried basil

Step-by-Step Directions to cook it:

1. Set your pot to sautéing, add

olive oil and let it heat up. Drop in the onions and cook them for about 3 minutes until translucent.

2. Sprinkle the basil into the pot and add the broth and tomatoes. Mix everything together, close the lid and seal the valve. Set the cooker for high pressure and the timer for 5 minutes.

3. After the time is up, let the pressure release naturally. When it's done, remove the lid from the pot and use an immersion blender blend the soup until very smooth.

4. Taste for seasoning. Add salt and pepper as needed.

5. Serve the soup warm, garnish with fresh basil leaves and a sprinkling of grated cheese (optionally).

Nutrition Facts Per Serving:

Calories 90, Fat 0 g, Carbs 20 g, Protein 2 g

Kale Soup

Kale soup is full of dark green kale, cannellini beans and potatoes. Best serve on a cold winter's night.
Prep time and cooking time: 21 minutes | Serves: 6

Ingredients To Use:

- 3 pounds of bone-in, skin-on chicken thighs
- 32 ounces of chicken broth
- 1 tablespoon of dried Italian seasoning
- 16 ounces of halved cremini mushrooms
- 1 chopped large bunch of kale (stems removed)

Step-by-Step Directions to cook it:

1. First, put the chicken into the pressure cooker along with 4 cups of water. Close the lid and seal the valve. Set the cooking time for 20 minutes and the pressure to high. After that time, release the pressure manually, remove the lid and take the chicken out of the pot. Set it aside until it's cool enough to work with.

2. Remove the bones and the skin from the meat and shred the chicken. Using a fine mesh strainer, strain the broth and return it with the meat into the pot.

3. Add the rest of the ingredients along with some herbs if you wish. Close the cover back and again seal the vent. Cook under high pressure for 1 minute, then release the pressure manually. Taste for seasoning, add salt and pepper as needed and serve.

Calories: 573, Fat: 32 g, Carbs: 11 g, Protein: 62 g

Split Pea & Ham Soup

These split pea and ham soup are great for lunches or dinner. With a flavor of sweet and salty, this recipe is the ideal fall or winter soup.
Prep time and cooking time: 25 minutes | Serves: 8

Ingredients To Use:

- 3 cups of green split peas
- 8 cups of chicken broth
- 1 thinly sliced celery stalk
- 1 diced yellow onion
- 3 minced cloves of garlic

Step-by-Step Directions to cook it:

1. Set the pressure cooker to sautéing and drizzle in some olive oil. Once it heats up, add the garlic, onion and celery and fry for 4-5 minutes, or until softened.
2. Pour in the broth and ass the peas. Season with salt and pepper and stir gently.
3. Seal the lid and the valve. Choose the soup setting on the Air fryer and cook for 15 minutes on high pressure.
4. As the time is up, quickly release the pressure and carefully remove the lid. Stir the soup,

taste for seasoning and adjust as needed. It's ready to serve!

Nutritional value per serving:

Calories: 181, Fat: 2.5 g, Carbs: 30.2 g, Protein: 10.1 g

Bountiful Bone Broth

Perfect for sauces, soups, and more, this bountiful bone broth is so flavorful and tasty.
Prep time and cooking time: 123 minutes | Serves: 12

Ingredients To Use:

- 1 cooked chicken carcass and drippings, with most of the meat removed
- 1 quartered small onion with skin on
- 2 whole cloves of garlic
- 2 tablespoons of apple cider vinegar
- 3-4 litters of filtered water

Step-by-Step Directions to cook it:

1. Place all solid ingredients into the pressure cooker. Fill the pot with filtered water until it reaches the 4-liter mark. Close the lid and seal the valve.
2. Set the pressure to high and the timer for 60 minutes. After that time, allow the pressure to release naturally.
3. Let the broth cool for about one hour. Once it is just warm, use a

spider or a slotted spoon to remove the solid ingredients into another container. Taste the broth for seasoning and adjust with salt and pepper as necessary.

4. Chill the broth for a couple of hours – it's best to let it chill overnight.

5. You can store the broth in smaller containers. It will remain fresh for a week in a fridge, or even up to 3 months in the freezer. When you want to use it, skim the fat that will solidify at the top.

Nutritional value per serving:

Calories: 40, Fat: 2.2 g, Carbs: 1.6 g, Protein: 4 g

Butternut Swirly Squash Soup

Butternut swirly squash soup is perfect for using up leftover turkey. Best serve on cold winter day. Prep time and cooking time: 22 minutes | Serves: 8

Ingredients To Use:

- 1 peeled and diced onion
- 2 pounds of diced butternut squash
- 1 peeled zucchini, cut into chunks

Step-by-Step Directions to cook it:

1. Use the sauté option to heat up some light oil in the pot. Place the onions inside and let them just become golden brown. Then, add the zucchini, diced squash and about 3 cups of water.

2. Close the lid and seal the valve. Set the pressure to high and cook for 15 minutes.

3. Unseal the valve to manually release the pressure. Blend with an immersion blender until the soup is smooth. Taste for seasoning, adjust and serve.

Nutritional value per serving:

Calories 126; Fat 9 g; Carbs 12 g; Protein 3 g

Lambast Lamb Stew

With potatoes, carrots and chunks of lamb. Lambast lamb stew is a delicious and satisfying recipe. Prep time and cooking time: 40 minutes | Serves: 8

Ingredients To Use:

- 2 pounds of lamb stew bits
- 1 peeled, seeded and cubed acorn squash
- 1 peeled and quartered yellow onion
- 1 sprig of fresh rosemary
- 6 finely sliced garlic cloves

Step-by-Step Directions to cook it:

1. Prepare your vegetables. Adjust their size depending on their firmness.
2. Add everything into the Air fryer with extra 3 tablespoons of water. Use the soup or stew function, at high pressure, for 5-6 minutes.
3. Let the pressure come down on its own once the time is up. Remove the lid, stir the soup, taste for seasoning and adjust as needed. It's ready to serve!

Nutritional value per serving:

Calories 382; Fat 13 g; Carbs 11 g; Protein 54 g

Royal Red Pepper Bisque

Royal red pepper bisque is a simple soup consisting of ripe red peppers in a creamy base.
Prep time and cooking time: 27 minutes | Serves: 8

Ingredients To Use:

- 1 chopped cauliflower head
- 2-3 minced garlic cloves
- 4 cups of vegetable broth
- 2 jars of roasted red peppers in water
- 1 6-ounce can of tomato paste

Step-by-Step Directions to cook it:

1. Heat up some olive oil (or other light cooking oil) using the sauté setting. When it's hot, put in the garlic and chopped cauliflower. Sauté them together, stirring from time to time, until the garlic begins to take on some color.
2. Turn the sautéing off. Add the rest of the ingredients to the pot, season with some salt and pepper. Add dried parsley or other herbs as you wish.
3. Close the lid and seal the valve. Set the cooker to the manual function and cook for 7 minutes. After the beep, manually quickly release the pressure.
4. Take off the lid carefully. With a blender, puree the soup until it's smooth and creamy. You can use either an immersion blender for easiest process. If you use a cup blender, you might need to do it in batches.
5. When the soup is smooth, taste for seasoning and adjust as needed. For extra flavor, stir in 6-8 ounces of crumbled goat cheese. Serve in warm bowls with a bit of yogurt (Greek works great) and a sprinkle of fresh herbs.

Nutritional value per serving:

Calories: 168, Fat: 11 g, Carbs: 10 g, Protein: 11 g

Chapter 7: Rice, Multi-grain, and Porridges

Rice, Almonds and Raisins Pudding

This recipe results in a delicacy fit for kings. The Instant Pot Duo Crisp Air Fryer Lid is a premium rice cooker.
Prep time and cooking time: 15 minutes | Serves: 4

Ingredients To Use:

- 1 cup of brown rice
- 1/2 cup of coconut chips
- 1 cup of milk
- 2 cups of water
- 1/2 cup of maple syrup
- 1/4 cup of raisins
- 1/4 cup of almonds
- A pinch of cinnamon powder

Step-by-Step Directions to Cook It:

1. Add the rice to a springform pan that fits the Instant Pot cooker base, stir in the water and cover with the Instant Pot Duo Crisp Air Fryer Lid.
2. Select the Broil Smart Program and set the timer for 15 minutes at 350°F.
3. Drain the rice, then add the raisins, almonds, maple syrup, cinnamon, and stir.
4. Replace the Instant Pot Duo Crisp Air Fryer Lid and reset the time to 8 minutes at the same Smart Program and temperature.
5. Serve the rice puddings into bowls.

Nutritional value per serving:

Calories: 251kcal, Fat: 6g, Carbs: 39g, Protein: 12g

Rice and Sausage Side Dish

An exquisite side dish that will improve your appetite and leave you hungry for more.
Prep time and cooking time: 30 minutes | Serves: 4

Ingredients To Use:

- 2 cups of white rice, boiled
- 1 Tbsp. butter
- Salt and black pepper, as desired
- 4 garlic cloves, grated
- 1 pork sausage, sliced
- 2 Tbsp. carrot, chopped
- 3 Tbsp. cheddar cheese, shredded
- 2 Tbsp. mozzarella cheese, grated

1. Set the empty cooker base to Sauté mode at 350°F and melt the butter. Stir in the garlic and brown for about 2 minutes.
2. Stir in the sausage, carrots, rice, pepper, and salt. Cover with the broil/dehydration tray and the Instant Pot Duo Crisp Air Fryer Lid.
3. Select the Broil Smart Program and set the timer for 10 minutes at 350°F.
4. Top with the mozzarella and cheddar and serve.

Nutritional value per serving:

Calories: 240kcal, Fat: 12g, Carbs: 20g, Protein: 13g

Blueberry and Brown Sugar Oatmeal

This is an incredibly easy recipe that can serve as a breakfast or a quick snack. Try it now with the Instant Pot Duo Crisp Air Fryer Lid.
Prep time and cooking time: 20 minutes | Serves: 4

Ingredients To Use:

- 1 cup of traditional rolled oats
- 1/2 tsp. cinnamon
- 1/2 tsp. of baking powder
- 1 medium egg
- 1/2 tsp. of nutmeg
- 1 cup of milk
- 3/4 cup of brown sugar
- Cooking spray

Step-by-Step Directions to Cook It:

1. Add the egg and milk to a bowl and whisk until well-combined.
2. Grease an oven-safe baking dish with the cooking spray and set aside.
3. In a separate bowl, mix the oats, cinnamon, brown sugar, nutmeg, and baking powder.
4. To the greased baking dish, add a quarter of the berries. This will serve as the bottom layer.
5. Add the entire egg mix. This will serve as the second layer.
6. Add the entire oat mix. This will serve as the third layer.
7. Cover the layers with the rest of the berries. Allow to rest for 10 minutes before transferring to the air fryer.
8. Cover with the Instant Pot Duo Crisp Air Fryer Lid and select the Bake Smart Program. Set the timer to 10 minutes at 320°F.
9. Slice and serve.

Nutritional value per serving:

Calories: 154kcal, Fat: 11g, Carbs: 15g, Protein: 8g

Wide Rice Pilaf

The wild rice is seasoned with spices, vegetables, and nuts, then transferred to the air fryer to boil and absorb the delectable taste of the chicken stock.

Prep time and cooking time: 35 minutes | Serves: 12

Ingredients To Use:

- 1 shallot, sliced
- 1 tsp. garlic, grated
- A drizzle of olive oil
- 1 cup of faro
- 3/4 cup of wild rice
- 4 cups of chicken stock
- Salt and black pepper, as desired
- 1 Tbsp. of chopped parsley
- 1/2 cup of toasted, chopped hazelnuts
- 3/4 cup of dried cherries
- Chopped chives, garnish

Step-by-Step Directions to Cook It:

1. In an oven-proof baking dish, mix the garlic, oil, shallots, faro, rice, salt, black pepper, parsley, cherries, stock, and hazelnuts.
2. Transfer the dish to the Instant Pot Air fryer basket and cover with the broil/dehydration tray and the Instant Pot Duo Crisp Air Fryer Lid.
3. Select the Broil Smart Program and set the timer for 25 minutes at 350°F.

4. Divide into equal portions and serve.

Nutritional value per serving:

Calories: 142kcal, Fat: 4g, Carbs: 16g, Protein: 4g

Pumpkin Rice

This meal can serve as a side dish or a main meal when you are interested in having a light lunch.

Prep time and cooking time: 35 minutes | Serves: 4

Ingredients To Use:

- 2 Tbsp. olive oil
- 1 small yellow onion, sliced
- 2 garlic cloves, grated
- 12 ounces of white rice
- 4 cup of chicken stock
- 6 ounces of pumpkin puree
- 1/2 tsp. nutmeg
- 1 tsp. of chopped thyme
- 1/2 tsp. of grated ginger
- 1/2 tsp. cinnamon powder
- 1/2 tsp. of allspice
- 4 ounces of heavy cream

Step-by-Step Directions to Cook It:

1. In an oven-proof baking dish, mix the rice, stock, oil, onion, pumpkin puree, garlic, nutmeg, ginger, thyme, cinnamon, cream, and allspice.
2. Transfer the pan to the Instant pot's air fryer basket and cover with the broil/dehydration tray

and the Instant Pot Duo Crisp Air Fryer Lid.

3. Select the Broil Smart Program and set the timer for 30 minutes at 360°F.
4. Divide into equal portions and serve as a side dish.

Nutritional value per serving:

Calories: 261kcal, Fat: 6g, Carbs: 19g, Protein: 4g

Wild Rice Soup

A spoon of this soup contains wild rice and a combination of spices that will cause an explosion of flavor in your mouth.
Prep time and cooking time: 1 hour | Serves: 8

Ingredients To Use:

- 1/3 cup of uncooked wild rice
- 1 Tbsp. vegetable oil
- 1/2 cup of butter
- 1 medium onion, thinly sliced
- 1 celery stalk, chopped
- 1 carrot, finely chopped
- 1/2 cup of all-purpose flour
- 3 cups of chicken stock
- 2 cups of half-and-half
- 1/2 tsp. of dried rosemary
- 1 tsp. salt

Step-by-Step Directions to Cook It:

1. Wash the rice and drain it.
2. Add the rice, oil, and 1 quart of water to the Instant Pot cooker base and cover with the Instant Pot Duo Crisp Air Fryer Lid.
3. Select the Broil Smart Program and set the timer for 30 minutes at 300°F.
4. After the rice is done, transfer the contents of the air fryer to a bowl.
5. Melt the butter in the now-empty cooker base, and sauté the celery, onion, and carrot until they are tender.
6. Stir in the flour and cook for another 3 minutes. Stir in the stock, rosemary, half and half, and boiled rice. Cover the air fryer with the Instant Pot Duo Crisp Air Fryer Lid and set the timer for 20 minutes at the same temperature and Smart program.

Nutritional value per serving:

Calories: 217kcal, Fat: 13g, Carbs: 17g, Protein: 10g

Rice Stuffed Bell Pepper Soup

Pamper your palates with this delicious treat. The bell peppers are stuffed with well-spiced and tasty rice.
Prep time and cooking time: | Serves: 16

Ingredients To Use:

- 1 pound of ground beef
- 4 cups of tomato juice

- 3 red or green bell peppers, cored, diced
- 1-1/2 cups of chili sauce
- 1 cup of long-grain rice
- 2 celery stalks, chopped
- 1 large onion, sliced
- 3 chicken bouillon cubes
- 2 garlic cloves, grated
- 1/2 tsp. salt
- 2 tsp. browning sauce
- Salt and black pepper, as desired

Step-by-Step Directions to Cook It:

1. Season the beef with the salt and black pepper before transferring to the air fryer basket and covering with the Instant Pot Duo Crisp Air Fryer Lid.
2. Select the Air Fry Smart Program and use the default timer.
3. When the beef is ready, add the stock, peppers, tomato juice, celery, rice, onion, chili sauce, bouillon cubes, browning sauce, salt, and 8 cups of water.
4. Replace the Instant Pot Duo Crisp Air Fryer Lid and select the Dehydrate Smart Program and set the timer for 1 hour at 300°F.
5. Divide into equal portions and serve.

Nutritional value per serving:

Calories: 157kcal, Fat: 8g, Carbs: 12g, Protein: 6g

Fresh Baked Oatmeal

Oatmeals always turn out great when prepared with the help of the Instant Pot Duo Crisp Air Fryer Lid. Try out this meal to experience the fantastic taste.

Prep time and cooking time: 30 minutes | Serves: 4

Ingredients To Use:

- 1 cup of milk
- 1/6 cup of brown sugar
- 1 large egg
- 2 cups of strawberries, halved
- 1 cup of traditionally rolled oats
- 1/2 tsp. of ground cinnamon
- 1/3 tsp. of salt
- 1/2 tsp. of baking powder
- 1/8 cup of slivered almonds
- Cooking spray

Step-by-Step Directions to Cook It:

1. Add the egg and milk to a bowl and whisk until well-combined.
2. In a medium bowl, mix the oats, sugar, baking powder, salt, and cinnamon. Stir thoroughly until well-combined.
3. Grease an oven-safe baking dish with the cooking spray and set aside.
4. Arrange a quarter of the strawberries at the bottom of the dish, layer with the oats mix, then the egg mix, and finally top with

the rest of the berries.

5. Allow to rest for 10 minutes, then sprinkle with nutmeg and almonds.
6. Transfer the dish to the Instant Pot cooker base, cover with the Instant Pot Duo Crisp Air Fryer Lid and select the Bake Smart Program.
7. Set the timer for 10 minutes at 320°F.
8. Allow to cool, slice, and serve.

Calories: 153kcal, Fat: 11g, Carbs: 9g, Protein: 7g

Instant pot Congee

This is an easy to make rice porridge that does not require attending to and there is no worry of burnt bottom or messy cleanup
Prep Time and Cooking Time: 60 minutes| Serves: 6

Ingredients to use:

- 3/4 cup jasmine rice
- 6 chicken drumsticks
- 1 tbsp. ginger
- 7 cups cold water
- Salt to taste
- Green onions

Step-by-step Directions to Cook It:

1. Wash and rinse the rice until the rice water is clear.

2. Pour the rice in the instant pot and add chicken, ginger, water, and salt.
3. Close the lid and pressure cook at high pressure for 30 minutes. Release the pressure naturally.
4. Turn on instant pot sauté function and stir the porridge until the desired consistency.
5. Shred the chicken using the fork and remove the bones and skin.
6. Remove from heat and serve immediately garnished with green onions

Calories: 186kcal, Carbs: 19g Fat: 6g, Protein: 13g

Breakfast Porridge

There is nothing amazing like kicking off the day with a delicious and filling breakfast. This porridge is a solid choice for a great breakfast.
Prep Time and Cooking Time: 23 minutes| Serves: 4

Ingredients to use:

- 3/4 cup steel cut oats
- 1/4 cup quinoa. Rinsed and drained
- 1/4 cup cranberries, dried
- 1/4 cup raisins
- 3 tbsp. flax seeds, ground
- 2 tbsp. chia seeds
- 1 tbsp. olive oil
- 1/4 tbsp. cinnamon, ground
- 1/4 tbsp. salt

- 2-1/2 cups almond milk
- 1-1/2 cups water
- Maple syrup
- 1/4 cup almonds, sliced

Step-by-step Directions to Cook It:

1. Spray a heatproof bowl with cooking spray.
2. Combine the oats, quinoa, cranberries, raisins, flax seeds, chia seeds, olive oil, cinnamon, and salt in the bowl.
3. Stir well to combine. Stir in milk until well blended.
4. Pour water in the instant pot and place a rack. Place the bowl on the rack and seal the lid. Cook for 13 minutes on high pressure.
5. Release pressure naturally. Open the lid and stir the porridge until smooth.
6. Serve the porridge with more almond milk, maple syrup, cranberries, and almonds.

Nutritional value per serving:

Calories: 189kcal, Carbs: 29g Fat: 76g, Protein: 15g

Instant pot porridge

This is an amazing porridge recipe that makes it easy to whip up an ick off your morning in a brilliant way.
Prep Time and Cooking Time: 16 minutes| Serves: 4

Ingredients to use:

- 1 tbsp. coconut oil
- 2/3 cup porridge or steel-cut oats
- 2 cups water

Step-by-step Directions to Cook It:

1. Place coconut oil in the instant pot.
2. Add porridge and water then give a good stir.
3. Seal the instant pot with lid and set time for 15 minutes on high pressure. Release pressure quickly
4. Remove the lid and divide the porridge among bowls.
5. Serve with the toppings and enjoy.

Nutritional value per serving:

Calories: 112kcal, Carbs: 17g Fat: 2g, Protein: 4g

Green Rice Porridge

This is a life-changing porridge that you will love. The porridge incorporates a lot of spinach making it super healthy
Prep Time and Cooking Time: 1 hour 35 minutes| Serves: 10

Ingredients to use:

- 1 cup jasmine rice, brown
- 1/2 cup jasmine rice, white
- 9 cups of water
- 1 tbsp. sea salt, fine grain

- 1/4 lb. chopped spinach

1. Combine the rice, water, and salt in the instant pot.
2. Seal the instant pot with the lid and set time for 30 minutes on high pressure.
3. Let the instant pot release pressure naturally for 40 minutes. Shake and tap the instant pot then open it.
4. Stir in spinach and serve the porridge topped with your favorite toppings.

Nutritional value per serving:

Calories: 102kcal, Carbs: 21g Fat: -g, Protein: 2g

Instant pot Butternut squash Rice Porridge

This is a simple, light, and above all very delicious butternut squash rice porridge that will blow you away. This porridge will be a hit in your home. Prep Time and Cooking Time: 26 minutes| Serves: 6

Ingredients to use:

- 2 tbsp. grass-fed butter
- 1 cup white rice, organic and long grain
- 1 cup butternut squash, shredded
- 1/2 cup raisins
- 1/2 tbsp. sea salt
- 3 tbsp. coconut sugar
- 1/2 tbsp. cinnamon, ground
- 3 cups milk, dairy-free

Step-by-step Directions to Cook It:

1. Press sauté function on the instant pot.
2. Melt the butter and add rice. Stir until all grains are well coated with butter.
3. Add butternut squash, raisins, salt, coconut sugar, cinnamon, and milk in the instant pot. Stir well to combine.
4. Seal the lid and cook for 6 minutes on high pressure.
5. When cooking is done, let rest for 10 minutes before naturally releasing pressure.
6. Open the lid, stir the porridge, and adjust salt and sugar.
7. Serve immediately.

Nutritional value per serving:

Calories: 231kcal, Carbs: 43g Fat: 6g, Protein: 3g

Mushroom Congee

This is great rice porridge to serve your family for breakfast. It's gentle on the stomach so perfect for the young ones. Top this porridge with your favorite toppings. Prep Time and Cooking Time: 8 hours 15 minutes| Serves: 6

- 8 cups of water
- 4 cups sliced shiitake mushrooms
- 4 cups mushrooms, sliced
- 1 cup of brown rice
- 3 tbsp. ginger, grated

Step-by-step Directions to Cook It:

1. Prepare mushrooms and ginger then store them in the fridge.
2. Add water, mushrooms, brown rice and ginger in the instant pot. Slow cook for 7-9 hours.
3. Serve the porridge with your favorite toppings. Enjoy.

Nutritional value per serving:

Calories: 97kcal, Carbs: 17g Fat: 2g, Protein: 5g

Vegetable Fried Rice

This is one of the best side dishes to serve in place of the usual plain rice. It's great, healthy and everyone will love it.
Prep Time and Cooking Time: 20 minutes| Serves: 4

Ingredients to use:

- 2 tbsp. sesame oil
- 2 cups of leftover rice
- 1/2 cup onions, diced
- 1 cup vegetable medley
- 2 tbsp. soy sauce
- 2 tbsp. sesame oil

- 2 eggs, beaten

Step-by-step Directions to Cook It:

1. Place oil in an air fryer safe pan.
2. Add rice and onions then give a good mix until the rice is well coated.
3. Stir in vegetable medley then toss until well coated. Place the pan in the air fryer basket and place the basket in the instant pot.
4. Select air fry and set temperature 320F and timer for 10 minutes. When halfway cooked mix well.
5. Add soy sauce and more oil .pour the egg over the rice and mix well. Air fry for 7 minutes.
6. Serve immediately.

Nutritional value per serving:

Calories: 379kcal, Carbs: 76g Fat: 3g, Protein: 17g

Instant Pot Air fryer Lid Rice

This is a quite versatile rice dish that you will love. It can be cooked with turkey pork or generally avoid meat.
Prep Time and Cooking Time: 25 minutes| Serves: 6

Ingredients to use:

- 3 cups cold rice
- 1 cup chicken

- 5 tbsp. tamari soy sauce
- 1-1/2 cup veggies, frozen
- 2 green onions, sliced
- 1 tbsp. sesame oil
- 1 tbsp. vegetable oil
- 1 tbsp. chili sauce
- Salt to taste

Step-by-step Directions to Cook It:

1. Mix all ingredients in a large mixing bowl then transfer to an air fryer safe pan.
2. Place the pan in an air fryer basket then place the basket in the instant pot.
3. Seal the instant pot with an air fryer lid and set the temperature to 350F and the timer for 20 minutes.
4. Mix the rice a couple of times while cooking. Serve immediately.

Nutritional value per serving:

Calories: 420kcal, Carbs: 80g Fat: 2g, Protein: 15g

Yummy Cheesy Rice Balls

Stuffed with glorious gooey cheese, this yummy cheesy rice balls are loved by children and adults.
Prep time and cooking time: 40 minutes | Serves: 1

Ingredients To Use:

- 1 cup rice [boiled]
- 1 cup paneer
- 1 tablespoon corn flour
- 1 green chili; chopped
- 1 cup cheese mozzarella; cubed
- 2 tablespoon carrot; chopped
- 2 tablespoon sweet corn
- 1 tablespoon corn flour slurry
- salt to taste
- garlic powder [optional] to taste
- 1/2 breadcrumbs
- 1 teaspoon oregano

Step-by-Step Directions to cook it:

1. Preheat Air Fryer to 390 - degrees Fahrenheit.
2. Mix all the above-mentioned ingredients and form into small ball shape.
3. Roll the mixture in slurry and breadcrumbs. Cook for 15 minutes.

Nutritional value per serving:

Calories 190; Fat 2 g; Carbs 23 g; Protein 8 g

Rice Flour Coated Shrimp

Mixed with rice and shrimp, you can make an incredible and delicious fried rice in no time.
Prep time and cooking time: 40 minutes | Serves: 3

Ingredients To Use:

- 3 tablespoons rice flour
- 1 pound shrimp, peeled and deveined
- 2 tablespoons olive oil

- 1 teaspoon powdered sugar
- Salt and black pepper, as required

1. Preheat the Air fryer to 325 o F and grease an Air fryer basket.
2. Mix rice flour, olive oil, sugar, salt, and black pepper in a bowl.
3. Stir in the shrimp and transfer half of the shrimp to the Air fryer basket.
4. Cook for about 10 minutes, flipping once in between.
5. Dish out the mixture onto serving plates and repeat with the remaining mixture.

Nutritional value per serving:

Calories: 299, Fat: 12g, Carbs: 11.1g, Protein: 35g

Rice in Crab Shell

Yummy fresh, tasty, delicious, bulky, and tasty soy-seasoned crabs. Best serve in lunch or dinner.
Prep time and cooking time: 28 minutes | Serves: 2

Ingredients To Use:

- 1 bowl cooked rice
- 4 tablespoons crab meat
- 2 tablespoons butter
- 2 tablespoons Parmesan cheese, shredded
- 2 crab shells
- Paprika, to taste

Step-by-Step Directions to cook it:

1. Preheat the Air fryer to 390 o F and grease an Air fryer basket.
2. Mix rice, crab meat, butter and paprika in a bowl.
3. Fill crab shell with rice mixture and top with Parmesan cheese.
4. Arrange the crab shell in the Air fryer basket and cook for about 8 minutes.
5. Sprinkle with more paprika and serve hot.

Nutritional value per serving:

Calories: 285, Fat: 33g, Carbs: 0g, Protein: 33g

Salmon and Jasmine Rice

The teriyaki glaze gives the fish a sweet taste, turning everyone into salmon lovers. Best serve on lunch.
Prep time and cooking time: 35 minutes | Serves: 2

Ingredients To Use:

- 2 wild salmon fillets; boneless
- 1/2 cup jasmine rice
- 1 tbsp. butter; melted
- 1/4 tsp. saffron
- 1 cup chicken stock
- Salt and black pepper to taste

Step-by-Step Directions to cook it:

1. Add all ingredients except the fish to a pan that fits your air

fryer; toss well

2. Place the pain in the air fryer and cook at 360°F for 15 minutes
3. Add the fish, cover and cook at 360°F for 12 minutes more. Divide everything between plates and serve right away.

Nutritional value per serving:

Calories 600; Fat 27 g; Carbs 50 g; Protein 38 g

Chicken with Veggies and Rice

Chicken with veggies and rice are a healthy weeknight dinner the whole family will love.
Prep time and cooking time: 35 minutes | Serves: 3

Ingredients To Use:

- 3 cups cold boiled white rice
- 1 cup cooked chicken, diced
- 1/2 cup frozen carrots
- 1/2 cup frozen peas
- 1/2 cup onion, chopped
- 6 tablespoons soy sauce
- 1 tablespoon vegetable oil

Step-by-Step Directions to cook it:

1. Preheat the Air fryer to 360 o F and grease a 7" nonstick pan.
2. Mix the rice, soy sauce, and vegetable oil in a bowl.
3. Stir in the remaining ingredients and mix until well combined.
4. Transfer the rice mixture into the

pan and place in the Air fryer.

5. Cook for about 20 minutes and dish out to serve immediately.

Nutritional value per serving:

Calories: 405, Fat: 6.4g, Carbs: 63g, Protein: 21.7g

Chicken Fried Rice

Mixed with chicken and rice, you can make this delicious Chinese food recipe. Perfect for lunch and dinner.
Prep time and cooking time: 20 minutes | Serves: 3

Ingredients To Use:

- 1 cup chicken; cooked and diced
- 3 cups white rice; cooked
- 1 cup frozen peas and carrots
- 1/2 cup onion; diced
- 1 tbsp. vegetable oil
- 6 tbsp. soy sauce

Step-by-Step Directions to cook it:

1. Place white rice into the mixing bowl, adding the vegetable oil and the soy sauce. Mix thoroughly.
2. Then, add the frozen peas and carrots, diced onions and diced chicken. Mix thoroughly once more
3. Pour the rice mixture into the nonstick pan and place in air fryer. Cook at 360°F for 20 minutes. Once done, remove and serve.

Calories 512; Fat 18 g; Carbs 58 g; Protein 29 g

Veggie Rice

Mixed with vegetables and rice, you can make a healthy veggie rice that's good for the body.
Prep time and cooking time: 38 minutes | Serves: 2

Ingredients To Use:

- 2 cups cooked white rice
- 1 large egg, lightly beaten
- 1/2 cup frozen peas, thawed
- 1/2 cup frozen carrots, thawed
- 1/2 teaspoon sesame seeds, toasted
- 1 tablespoon vegetable oil
- 2 teaspoons sesame oil, toasted and divided
- 1 tablespoon water
- Salt and ground white pepper, as required
- 1 teaspoon soy sauce
- 1 teaspoon Sriracha sauce

Step-by-Step Directions to cook it:

1. Preheat the Air fryer to 380 o F and grease an Air fryer pan.
2. Mix the rice, vegetable oil, 1 teaspoon of sesame oil, water, salt, and white pepper in a bowl.
3. Transfer the rice mixture into the Air fryer basket and cook for about 12 minutes.

4. Pour the beaten egg over rice and cook for about 4 minutes.
5. Stir in the peas and carrots and cook for 2 more minutes.
6. Meanwhile, mix soy sauce, Sriracha sauce, sesame seeds and the remaining sesame oil in a bowl.
7. Dish out the potato cubes onto serving plates and drizzle with sauce to serve.

Nutritional value per serving:

Calories: 163, Fat: 8.4g, Carbs: 15.5g, Protein: 6.4g

Rice and Beans Stuffed Bell Peppers

Filled with onion, Mexican spices and rice. These rice and beans stuffed bell peppers are gluten free, low carb and a delicious meatless meal!
Prep time and cooking time: 30 minutes | Serves: 5

Ingredients To Use:

- 5 large bell peppers, tops removed and seeded
- 1/2 cup mozzarella cheese, shredded
- 1/2 small bell pepper, seeded and chopped
- 1-1/2 tsp. Italian seasoning
- 1: 15-ozcan red kidney beans, rinsed and drained
- 1: 15-ozcan diced tomatoes with juice

- 1 cup cooked rice
- 1 tbsp. Parmesan cheese; grated

Step-by-Step Directions to cook it:

1. In a bowl; mix well chopped bell pepper, tomatoes with juice, beans, rice and Italian seasoning. Stuff each bell pepper evenly with the rice mixture.
2. Set the temperature of air fryer to 360°F. Grease an air fryer basket.
3. Arrange bell peppers into the air fryer basket in a single layer.
4. Air fry for about 12 minutes. Meanwhile; in a bowl; mix together the mozzarella and Parmesan cheese.
5. Remove the air fryer basket and top each bell pepper with cheese mixture. Air fry for 3 more minutes.
6. Remove from air fryer and transfer the bell peppers onto a serving platter. Set aside to cool slightly. Serve warm.

Nutritional value per serving:

Calories 140; Fat 2 g; Carbs 27 g; Protein 7 g

Rice Flour Crusted Tofu

This tofu recipe is completely gorgeous. Mixed with rice flour, olive oil, cornstarch and salt and ground black pepper.

Prep time and cooking time: 43 minutes | Serves: 3

Ingredients To Use:

- 1: 14-ozblock firm tofu, pressed and cubed into ½-inch size
- 1/4 cup rice flour
- 2 tbsp. olive oil
- 2 tbsp. cornstarch
- Salt and ground black pepper; as your liking

Step-by-Step Directions to cook it:

1. In a bowl; mix together cornstarch, rice flour, salt and black pepper.
2. Coat the tofu evenly with flour mixture. Drizzle the tofu with oil.
3. Set the temperature of air fryer to 360°F. Grease an air fryer basket.
4. Arrange tofu cubes into the prepared air fryer basket in a single layer.
5. Air fry for about 14 minutes per side. Remove from air fryer and transfer the tofu onto serving plates. Serve warm.

Nutritional value per serving:

Calories 285; Fat 2 g; Carbs 19 g; Protein 17 g

Cauliflower Rice and Plum Pudding

Cauliflower rice and plum pudding is a delicious recipe. Mixed with coconut milk, ghee and stevia. Prep time and cooking time: 30 minutes | Serves: 4

Ingredients To Use:

- 4 plums, pitted and roughly chopped.
- 1-1/2 cups cauliflower rice
- 2 cups coconut milk
- 2 tbsp. ghee; melted
- 3 tbsp. stevia

Step-by-Step Directions to cook it:

1. Take a bowl and mix all the ingredients, toss, divide into ramekins, put them in the air fryer and cook at 340°F for 25 minutes.
2. Cool down and serve

Nutritional value per serving:

Calories: 221; Fat: 4g; Carbs: 3g; Protein: 3g

Chapter 8: Beans, Chilis, and Eggs

French Beans and Egg Breakfast Mix

The combination of beans and eggs is healthy and delicious. With the Instant Pot Duo Crisp Air Fryer Lid, you can eat healthily and deliciously. Prep time and cooking time: 30 minutes | Serves: 3

Ingredients To Use:

- 2 eggs, whisked
- 1/2 tsp. of soy sauce
- 1 Tbsp. olive oil
- 4 garlic cloves, minced
- 3 ounces of trimmed French beans
- Salt and white pepper, as desired

Step-by-Step Directions to Cook It:

1. Mix the eggs and soy sauce in a bowl. Season with salt and black pepper, then whisk thoroughly.
2. Set the empty cooker base to Sauté mode at 320˚F and heat the oil. Stir in the garlic and brown for about 1 minute.
3. Add the egg mix and French beans to the cooker base, cover with the Instant Pot Duo Crisp Air Fryer Lid and select the Broil Smart Program.
4. Set the timer for 10 minutes at the same temperature.
5. Divide into equal portions and serve.

Nutritional value per serving:

Calories: 182kcal, Fat: 3g, Carbs: 8g, Protein: 3g

Chicken, Beans, Corn and Quinoa Casserole

This isn't your regular casserole. The recipe is designed for people who enjoy beans in their quinoa casserole. Prep time and cooking time: 40 minutes | Serves: 8

Ingredients To Use:

- 1 cup of quinoa, cooked
- 3 cup of shredded chicken breast, cooked
- 14 ounces of canned black beans
- 12 ounces of corn
- 1/2 cup of chopped cilantro
- 6 kale leaves, chopped
- 1/2 cup of chopped green onions
- 1 cup of clean tomato sauce
- 1 cup of clean salsa
- 2 tsp. chili powder
- 2 tsp. of ground cumin
- 3 cups of shredded mozzarella cheese
- 1 Tbsp. garlic powder

- Cooking spray
- 2 jalapeno peppers, chopped

1. Lightly grease an oven-safe baking dish with the cooking spray.
2. To the dish, add the chicken, beans, kale, cilantro, green onions, cumin, quinoa, corn, salsa, garlic, chili powder, mozzarella, and jalapenos. Toss.
3. Transfer the baking dish to the Instant Pot cooker base and cover with the Instant Pot Duo Crisp Air Fryer Lid.
4. Select the Bake Smart Program and set the timer for 15 minutes at 350°F

Nutritional value per serving:

Calories: 365kcal, Fat: 12g, Carbs: 22g, Protein: 26g

Green Beans Side Dish

The green beans are seasoned and then air fried to give a crispy and delicious taste. This recipe is truly a marvel.
Prep time and cooking time: 35 minutes | Serves: 4

Ingredients To Use:

- 1-1/2 pound of trimmed green beans, steamed for 3 minutes
- Salt and black pepper, as desired
- 1/2 pound of chopped shallots

- 1/4 cup of toasted almonds
- 2 Tbsp. olive oil

Step-by-Step Directions to Cook It:

1. Mix the green beans, pepper, salt, shallots, oil, and almonds in the air fryer's basket. Toss well.
2. Transfer to the air fryer and cover with the Instant Pot Duo Crisp Air Fryer Lid.
3. Select the Air Fry Smart Program and set the timer for 2 minutes at 400°F.
4. Divide into equal portions and serve.

Nutritional value per serving:

Calories: 152kcal, Fat: 3g, Carbs: 7g, Protein: 4g

Cod Fillets and Peas

The cod is well-seasoned and then air-roasted to produce a tasty, crunchy, and exquisite meal.
Prep time and cooking time: 20 minutes | Serves: 4

Ingredients To Use:

- 4 boneless cod fillets
- 2 Tbsp. of chopped parsley
- 2 cups of peas
- 4 Tbsp. wine
- 1/2 tsp. of dried oregano
- 1/2 tsp. sweet paprika
- 2 garlic cloves, grated
- Salt and pepper, as desired

1. Add the garlic, parsley, oregano, salt, paprika, wine and black pepper to the food processor and pulse until a smooth mixture is obtained. This will serve as the rub
2. Coat the cod with the rub and place in the Instant Pot cooker base. Cover with the Instant Pot Duo Crisp Air Fryer Lid and select the Roast Smart Program.
3. Set the timer for 10 minutes at 360°F.
4. When ready, remove the fish and set it aside.
5. Add the pea to the now-empty Instant Pot cooker base and cover with water. Season with salt and cover with the Instant Pot Duo Crisp Air Fryer Lid.
6. Select the broil Smart Program and set the timer to 10 minutes at the same temperature.
7. Serve the fish with the peas and drizzle with the leftover rub

Nutritional value per serving:

Calories: 261kcal, Fat: 8g, Carbs: 20g, Protein: 22g

Ham and Eggs

If you have never tried to eat bread and ham together, you definitely don't know what you're missing. The bread is soaked with the egg, and this gives it a delicious hard, and crunchy taste when it is ready. Try this recipe out ASAP!

Prep time and cooking time: 24 minutes | Serves: 1

Ingredients To Use:

- 2 bread slices
- 1 egg white
- 1/2 lb. ham, sliced
- 1 tsp. sugar
- Salt and black pepper, as desired

Step-by-Step Directions to Cook It:

1. Arrange the bread slices together and slice them diagonally.
2. Whisk the egg white in a bowl and add the sugar.
3. Add the bread triangles in the bowl and allow them to absorb the egg mixture.
4. Transfer the coated bread to the air fryer basket.
5. Season the ham with salt and pepper, then transfer to the bottom of the air fryer.
6. Cover with the Instant Pot Duo Crisp Air Fryer Lid and select the Bake Smart Program for 24 minutes at 320°F.
7. Turn the bread triangles halfway for an even cook.
8. Transfer the bread and ham into plates and serve.

Calories: 89kcal, Fat: 8g, Carbs: 11g, Protein: 7g

Egg White Chips

This recipe can be described in three powerful words –easy, delicious, and fast.

Prep time and cooking time: 15 minutes | Serves: 2

Ingredients To Use:

- 1/2 Tbsp. water
- 2 Tbsp. parmesan, shredded
- 4 eggs whites
- Salt and black pepper, as desired

Step-by-Step Directions to Cook It:

1. Whisk the egg whites in a bowl, then add the salt, black pepper, and water.
2. Scoop the mixture to a pre-prepared muffin pan and transfer it to the air fryer.
3. Cover with the Instant Pot Duo Crisp Air Fryer Lid and select the Bake Smart Program. Set the timer for 8 minutes at 350°F
4. Transfer to plates and serve

Nutritional value per serving:

Calories: 180kcal, Fat: 2g, Carbs: 12g, Protein: 7g

Scrambled Eggs

Who doesn't love a good scrambled egg recipe? The spices used in this recipe are not regular, neither is the appliance used for cooking it. Try it out now to experience the extraordinary taste.

Prep time and cooking time: 10 minutes | Serves: 2

Ingredients To Use:

- 2 large eggs
- 2 Tbsp. butter
- Green onions, as desired
- Salt and black pepper, as desired
- 1 red bell pepper, chopped
- A pinch of sweet paprika

Step-by-Step Directions to Cook It:

1. Mix the eggs, paprika, salt, black pepper, bell pepper, and green onions in a bowl.
2. Preheat the Instant Pot cooker base to 140°F and melt the butter.
3. Cover with the Instant Pot Duo Crisp Air Fryer Lid, select the Air Fry Smart Program and set the timer for 6 minutes at the 140°F.
4. Scrape the eggs from the air fryer and serve.

Nutritional value per serving:

Calories: 200kcal, Fat: 4g, Carbs: 10g, Protein: 3g

Fast Eggs and Tomatoes

You can have this meal on your plate within 10 minutes. It is fast, it is easy, and it is worth all the fuss.

Prep time and cooking time: 15 minutes | Serves: 4

Ingredients To Use:

- 4 large eggs
- 2 ounces of milk
- 2 Tbsp. of grated parmesan, grated
- Cooking spray
- Salt and black pepper, as desired
- 8 cherry tomatoes, halved

Step-by-Step Directions to Cook It:

1. Lightly grease the Instant Pot cooker base with the cooking spray and preheat to 200°F.
2. Mix the eggs, cheese, salt, pepper, and milk in a bowl.
3. Transfer the egg mixture to the preheated air fryer and cover it with the Instant Pot Duo Crisp Air Fryer Lid.
4. Select the Bake Smart program and set the timer for 6 minutes at the same temperature.
5. Add the tomatoes to the air fryer and cook for another 3 minutes.
6. Divide into equal portions and serve.

Nutritional value per serving:

Calories: 200kcal, Fat: 4g, Carbs: 12g, Protein: 3g

Egg White Omelettes

Without the yolk and with the addition of the skimmed milk, the omelets are pure white and delicious.

Prep time and cooking time: 25 minutes | Serves: 4

Ingredients To Use:

- 1 cup of egg whites
- 1/4 cup of chopped tomato
- 2 Tbsp. of skimmed milk
- 1/4 cup of green onions, chopped
- 2 Tbsp. of chopped chives
- Salt and black pepper, as desired

Step-by-Step Directions to Cook It:

1. Mix the egg whites, milk, tomato, onions, chives, salt, and black pepper in the Instant Pot cooker base.
2. Cover with the Instant Pot Duo Crisp Air Fryer Lid and select the Bake Smart Program.
3. Cook for 15 minutes at 320°F.
4. Allow to cool, then slice and serve into plates.

Nutritional value per serving:

Calories: 100kcal, Fat: 3g, Carbs: 7g, Protein: 4g

Lunch Egg Rolls

This is an egg roll recipe with an advanced degree. Try it out now to experience the burst of flavor that comes with baking vegetables and eggs together.

Prep time and cooking time: 25 minutes | Serves: 4

Ingredients To Use:

-
- 1/2 cup of chopped mushrooms
- 1/2 cup of carrots, grated
- 1/2 cup of grated zucchini
- 2 green onions, sliced
- 2 Tbsp. soy sauce
- 8 egg roll wrappers
- 1 egg, beaten
- 1 Tbsp. cornstarch

Step-by-Step Directions to Cook It:

1. Mix the carrots, zucchini, mushrooms, soy sauce, and onions in a bowl.
2. Place the egg wrappers on a flat surface and arrange the veggie mix in them. Afterward, roll the wrappers.
3. Mix the cornstarch and egg in a bowl and use it to coat the egg wrappers.
4. Seal the edges of the wrapper and transfer them to the Instant Pot cooker base.
5. Cover with the Instant Pot Duo Crisp Air Fryer Lid and select the Bake Smart Program and set the timer for 15 minutes at 370°F
6. Transfer to a platter and serve.

Nutritional value per serving:

Calories: 172kcal, Fat: 6g, Carbs: 8g, Protein: 7g

Egg Soufflé

This is an easy breakfast recipe that keeps everyone satisfied in the morning. When prepared in an Instant Pot Duo Crisp air fryer lid, it is perfectly tasty for breakfast yummiest.

Prep time and cooking time: 18 minutes| Serves: 2

Ingredients to use:

- 2 eggs
- 1 tbsp. chopped parsley, fresh
- 1/4 tbsp. garlic powder
- Pepper
- 2 tbsp. heavy cream
- Salt

Step-by-Step Directions to Cook It:

1. Spray cooking spray in 4 ramekins and set aside.
2. In the meantime, whisk eggs, parsley, garlic powder, pepper, cream, and salt in a bowl.
3. Pour the mixture into the ramekins.
4. Place a dehydrating tray in an air fryer basket, multi-level, then place the basket in an instant pot.

5. Now place the ramekins on your dehydrating tray.
6. Seal your pot using an air fryer lid.
7. Set to air fry mode, temperature to 400°F and set the timer for 8 minutes
8. Serve.

Nutritional value per serving:

Calories: 117kcal, Carbs: 1.2g Fat: 9.9g, Protein: 6g

Baked Eggs

This baked egg satisfies your cravings. It is a super easy recipe to prepare as it requires less than 20 minutes from start to finish and involves 5 ingredients.
Prep time and cooking time: 18 minutes| Serves: 2

Ingredients to use:

- 2 eggs
- 1/4 tbsp. garlic powder
- 1/4 tbsp. parsley
- Salt
- Pepper
- 1/4 cup chopped spinach
- 1/4 diced onion

Step-by-Step Directions to Cook It:

1. Spray cooking spray into 2 ramekins.
2. Whisk eggs, garlic powder, parsley, salt and pepper in a bowl, small.
3. Add spinach and onions then stir well.
4. Now pour the egg mixture into the ramekins.
5. Place a dehydrating tray in an air fryer basket, multi-level, then place the basket in an instant pot.
6. Now place the ramekins on your dehydrating tray.
7. Seal your pot using an air fryer lid.
8. Set to air fry mode, temperature to 350°F and set the timer for 8 minutes
9. Serve and enjoy.

Nutritional value per serving:

Calories: 71kcal, Carbs: 2.1g Fat: 4.4g, Protein: 5.9g

Bacon Egg Muffins

This breakfast recipe is perfect for cold days. It is a healthy recipe that comes out perfectly and tastes amazing. Everyone including your kids will love it.
Prep time and Cooking time: 35 minutes| Serves: 12

Ingredients to use:

- 12 eggs
- 1/3 cup heavy cream
- 1/2 tbsp. mustard powder
- Salt
- Pepper
- 8 cooked bacon slices, crumbled
- 4 oz. shredded cheddar cheese
- 2 tbsp. chopped parsley, fresh
- 2 chopped green onions

Step-by-Step Directions to Cook It:

1. Whisk egg, heavy cream, mustard powder, salt, and pepper in a bowl, mixing.
2. Divide bacon slices, and cheddar cheese among 12 silicone muffin molds.
3. Pour the egg mixture equally among the 12 muffin molds.
4. Place a dehydrating tray in an air fryer basket, multi-level, then place the basket in an instant pot.
5. Now place 6 muffin molds on the dehydrating tray.
6. Seal your pot using an air fryer lid.
7. Set to air fry mode, temperature to 375°F and set the timer for 25 minutes
8. Serve and enjoy.

Nutritional value per serving:

Calories: 183kcal, Carbs: 1g Fat: 14.1g, Protein: 12.8g

Tomato Egg Muffins

This is a delicious recipe when prepared in an Instant Pot Duo Crisp air fryer lid. It is a healthy recipe as eggs are rich in lutein and zeaxanthin antioxidants which prevent macular degeneration and important for eye health.
Prep time and cooking time: 30 minutes| Serves: 6

Ingredients to use:

- 4 egg whites
- 2 eggs
- 1/2 cup almond milk
- Salt
- Pepper
- 1/4 cup shredded cheddar cheese
- 1/4 cup diced olives
- 1 tbsp. chopped parsley, fresh
- 1/4 cup diced tomatoes
- 1/4 cup diced onion

Step-by-Step Directions to Cook It:

1. Whisk egg whites, eggs, milk, salt, and pepper in a bowl, mixing.
2. Add cheese, olives, parsley, tomatoes, and onions then stir well.
3. Divide the egg mixture among 6 silicone muffin molds
4. Place a dehydrating tray in an air fryer basket, multi-level, then place the basket in an instant pot.
5. Now place the muffin molds on your dehydrating tray.
6. Seal your pot using an air fryer lid.
7. Set to air fry mode, temperature to 350°F and set the timer for 20 minutes
8. Serve and enjoy.

Nutritional value per serving:

Calories: 107kcal, Carbs: 2.6g Fat: 8.5g, Protein: 6.1g

Greek Egg Muffins

This is a delicious egg muffin made in an Instant Pot Duo Crisp air fryer lid.. It is a perfect choice for your breakfast. You will enjoy it.

Prep time and cook time: 30 minutes| Serves: 12

Ingredients to use:

- 6 eggs
- Salt
- Pepper
- 1/2 cup crumbled feta cheese
- 3 chopped grape tomatoes
- 4 chopped tomatoes, sun-dried
- 2 tbsp. olive oil

Step-by-Step Directions to Cook It:

1. Whisk eggs, salt, and pepper in a bowl.
2. Stir in all remaining ingredients.
3. Pour the egg mixture among 12 silicone muffin molds.
4. Place a dehydrating tray in an air fryer basket, multi-level, then place the basket in an instant pot.
5. Now place 6 muffin molds on your dehydrating tray.
6. Seal your pot using an air fryer lid.
7. Set to air fry mode, temperature to 350°F and set the timer for 20 minutes
8. Bake with the same method for the remaining muffin molds.
9. Serve and enjoy.

Nutritional value per serving:

Calories: 62kcal, Carbs: 2.1g Fat: 4.4g, Protein: 4g

Tomato Mushroom Frittata

Are you bored preparing a normal breakfast? The tomato mushroom frittata is a perfect breakfast switch. They are good for beginners as they are easy to prepare.

Prep time and cook time: 16 minutes| Serves: 2

Ingredients to use:

- 3 eggs
- 2 tbsp. milk
- 2 sliced mushrooms
- 2 tbsp. chopped tomato
- 3 tbsp. chopped onion
- Salt
- Pepper
- 2 tbsp. shredded cheddar cheese

Step-by-Step Directions to Cook It:

1. Whisk eggs and milk in a bowl.
2. Add mushrooms, tomato, onions, salt, and pepper then whisk well
3. Pour the mixture into a baking pan and top with cheese.
4. Place the baking pan on a steam rack then place the steam rack into an instant pot.
5. Seal your pot using an air fryer lid.
6. Set to air fry mode, temperature to 400°F and set the timer for 6 minutes

7. Serve and enjoy.

Nutritional value per serving:

Calories: 142kcal, Carbs: 3.8g Fat: 9.3g, Protein: 11.4g

Sweet Potato Bites

This recipe is very quick and easy to prepare. These sweet potato bites will keep you filled up thus making a perfect snack.

Prep time and cook time: 25 minutes| Serves: 2

Ingredients to use:

- 2 diced sweet potato, 1-inch cubes
- 2 tbsp. cinnamon
- 2 tbsp. honey
- 1 tbsp. olive oil
- Pepper
- Salt

Step-by-Step Directions to Cook It:

1. Place all ingredients in a bowl, mix, and toss well.
2. Use cooking spray to spray instant pot air fryer baskets, multi-level.
3. Place the mixture into the basket and place the basket in your instant pot.
4. Seal your pot using an air fryer lid.
5. Set to air fry mode, temperature to 400°F, and set the timer for 6 minutes. Stir halfway through.
6. Serve and enjoy.

Nutritional value per serving:

Calories: 233kcal, Carbs: 42.8g Fat: 7.2g, Protein: 2.5g

Veggie Omelet

The veggie omelet is delicious, easy to make, convenient, and the perfect way to enjoy breakfast. Can be prepared earlier and kids can carry for lunch.

Prep time and cook time: 20 minutes| Serves: 2

Ingredients to use:

- 2 eggs
- Pinch of salt
- 1/4 cup milk
- 1 tbsp. mixed herbs
- 1/4 cup chopped mushrooms
- 2 tbsp. chopped tomato
- 2 tbsp. chopped bell pepper
- 1/4 cup shredded cheddar cheese

Step-by-Step Directions to Cook It:

1. Whisk eggs, salt, milk, and herbs in a bowl, small, then add vegetables.
2. Pour the mixture into a baking pan then top with cheese.
3. Place the baking pan on a steam rack then place the steam rack into your instant pot.
4. Seal your pot using an air fryer lid.
5. Set to air fry mode, temperature to 350°F and set the timer for 10

minutes
6. Serve and enjoy.

Nutritional value per serving:

Calories: 178kcal, Carbs: 12g Fat: 10g, Protein: 11.7g

Tomato Pepper Frittata

This is a colorful and easy frittata to prepare in an Instant Pot Duo Crisp air fryer lid. It is delicious that your family will absolutely love it.
Prep time and cook time: 25 minutes| Serves: 2

Ingredients to use:

- 1 cup egg whites
- 1/4 cup sliced tomato
- 1/4 cup sliced pepper
- 2 tbsp milk
- Pepper
- Salt

Step-by-Step Directions to Cook It:

1. Place all ingredients in a bowl, large, then whisk until fully combined.
2. Pour the mixture into a baking dish.
3. Place the baking dish on a steam rack then place the steam rack into your instant pot.
4. Seal your pot using an air fryer lid.
5. Set to air fry mode, temperature to 320°F, and set the timer for 15 minutes.
6. Serve and enjoy.

Nutritional value per serving:

Calories: 87kcal, Carbs: 5.6g Fat: 0.7g, Protein: 14.5g

Healthy Kale Muffins

This is a delicious healthy lunch and requires 40 minutes to be ready. It is a healthy recipe as kale makes a perfect addition to a weight loss diet. The kale muffins can be made for a snack.
Prep time and cook time: 40 minutes| Serves: 8

Ingredients to use:

- 6 eggs, large
- 1/2 cup almond milk
- 1 cup chopped kale
- 1/4 cup chopped chives
- Pepper
- Salt

Step-by-step directions to cook it:

1. Place all ingredients in a bowl then whisk well.
2. Pour the mixture into 8 silicone muffin molds.
3. Place a dehydrating tray in an air fryer basket, multi-level, then place the basket in an instant pot.
4. Now place 6 muffin molds on your dehydrating tray.
5. Seal your pot using an air fryer lid.
6. Set to air fry mode, temperature to 350°F, and set the timer for 30 minutes.

7. Repeat process for the remaining muffin molds.
8. Serve and enjoy.

Calories: 93kcal, Carbs: 2.1g Fat: 7.3g, Protein: 5.4g

Instant Cheesy Bean Bake

The instant pot is the best way to prepare beans but with air fryer lid addition, the bar is raised. Topping the beans with cheese then boiling takes this recipe to the next level. Everyone will enjoy the appetizer
Prep time and cook time: 55 minutes|
Serves: 6

Ingredients to use:

- 2 tbsp. olive oil, extra-virgin
- 1-1/2 tbsp. minced garlic
- 3 tbsp. tomato paste
- 1-1/3 cups beans, dried
- Kosher salt
- Black pepper
- 1-1/3 cups coarsely grated mozzarella

Step-by-Step Directions to Cook It:

1. Wash the beans and put them in the inner pot. Pour 4 cups of water, cold, in.
2. Cover the pot and pressure cook on high for about 25 minutes. Quick-release pressure.
3. Take the beans out, drain, and set aside then rinse your inner pot.
4. Place the inner pot back and select sauté setting then add oil. Cook for 20-25 seconds then garlic and fry for about 1 minute until golden, lightly.
5. Add tomato paste and cook for an additional 30 seconds giving it a quick stir.
6. Add beans, pepper, and salt then stir to combine.
7. Now press the cancel button.
8. Splash with cheese and close with an air fryer lid.
9. Select the boil setting and set the timer to 7 minutes.
10. Serve with nacho chips.
11. Enjoy.

Nutritional value per serving:

Calories: 128kcal, Carbs: 9.5g Fat: 7.9g, Protein: 7g

Crispy Falafel

Making falafel is easy and healthy at the same time. When prepared in an instant pot air fryer lid, it comes out perfectly moist, inside is fluffy, and crispy outside. It is good for make-ahead and freezer friendly.
Prep time and cook time: 50 minutes|
Serves: 24

Ingredients to use:

- 2 cups chickpeas, dried
- 1 cup fresh parsley
- 1 onion, quartered
- 1/4 cup fresh cilantro, stem

removed
- 6 peeled garlic cloves
- 3/4 cup fresh dill leaves, stem removed
- Salt
- 1 tbsp. cumin powder
- 1 tbsp. baking powder
- 1 tbsp. coriander powder
- 1 tbsp. cayenne powder

Optional:

- 2 tbsp. sesame seeds
- 3 tbsp. olive oil

Step-by-Step Directions to Cook It:

1. Soak the chickpeas overnight.
2. Pat dry all ingredients using a kitchen towel.
3. Place chickpeas, parsley, cilantro, dill, cumin powder, cayenne powder, coriander powder, pepper, garlic, and onion in a food processor. Process until a coarse meal.
4. Transfer the mixture into a bowl, cover using a cling wrap, and refrigerate about 1-3 hours.
5. Add baking powder and salt mixing well.
6. Form patties, 2x1/2-inch, then coat them with oil.
7. Place a fryer basket on top of a trivet placed inside an instant pot.
8. Now arrange the coated patties with oil on the fryer basket.
9. Seal your pot using an air fryer lid.

10. Set the temperature to 350°F, and set the timer for 6 minutes. Flip and set for another 6 minutes until falafel is golden brown.
11. Serve and enjoy.

Nutritional value per serving:

Calories: 91kcal, Carbs: 12.5g Fat: 3.4g, Protein: 3.9g

Instant pot Air fryer Lid Green Beans with Bacon

This is an amazing keto dish that will be your new favorite. It's easy to cook and can be served as a side dish of your choice.
Prep Time and Cooking Time: 25 minutes| Serves: 4

Ingredients to use:

- 3 cups green beans, chopped
- 3 slices of bacon, diced
- 1/4 cup water
- 1 tbsp salt
- 1 tbsp black pepper, ground

Step-by-step Directions to Cook It:

1. Place the all ingredients in a tray and place the tray in the air fryer basket. Place the basket in the instant pot.
2. Close the instant pot with the air fryer lid and select air fry. Set the temperature to 375°F and the timer for 15 minutes.

3. Raise the temperature to 400⁰F and add 5 more minutes.
4. Let rest before serving. Enjoy.

Calories: 95kcal, Carbs: 6g Fat: 6g, Protein: 3g

Easy green beans

These green beans are a special and tasty vegetable treat to include in the main meals or serve as a snack. They are simple but very yummy.
Prep Time and Cooking Time: 8 minutes| Serves: 2

Ingredients to use:

- 1 lb. green beans
- Cooking spray
- salt

Step-by-step Directions to Cook It:

1. Add the beans in the air fryer basket and place the basket in the instant pot.
2. Spray the beans with cooking spray and season with salt.
3. Seal the instant pot with an air fryer lid and select the air fry setting.
4. Set the temperature to 400°F and the timer for 8 minutes. Turn a couple of times during the cooking so that they brown evenly.
5. Serve with chopped herbs and salt. Enjoy.

Nutritional value per serving:

Calories: 35kcal, Carbs: 7g Fat: -g, Protein: 2g

Garlic and Parmesan Green Beans Fries

This is a perfect healthy snack to serve on a movie night or on game night. You can whip up these green bean fries within a short time.
Prep Time and Cooking Time: 10 minutes| Serves: 6

Ingredients to use:

- 1 lb. green beans, fresh
- 1/2 cup flour
- 2 eggs
- 1 cup panko bread crumbs
- 1/2 cup Parmesan cheese
- 1 cup panko bread crumbs
- 1 tbsp. garlic powder

Step-by-step Directions to Cook It:

1. Wash and rinse the green beans. Coat them with flour if you desire.
2. In a mixing bowl, whisk eggs.
3. In a separate bowl, mix cheese, breadcrumbs, and garlic.
4. Dip the green beans in the eggs, then in the breadcrumbs mixture.
5. Place them in the air fryer basket. Place the basket in the instant pot and seal the instant pot using an air fryer lid.
6. Set the temperature to 400°F and

the timer for 5 minutes.
7. Sprinkle with more cheese and serve.

Nutritional value per serving:

Calories: 98kcal, Carbs: 14g Fat: 3g, Protein: 5g

Creamy Veggie Omelet

Use any type of cheese you like, these creamy veggie omelet is serve on top of toast.
Prep time and cooking time: 24 minutes | Serves: 4

Ingredients To Use:

- 4 eggs, beaten
- 1 tablespoon cream cheese
- 1/2 teaspoon chili flakes
- 1/2 cup broccoli florets, chopped
- 1/4 teaspoon salt
- 1/4 cup heavy cream
- 1/4 teaspoon white pepper
- Cooking spray

Step-by-Step Directions to cook it:

1. Put the beaten eggs in the big bowl.
2. Add chili flakes, salt, and white pepper.
3. With the help of the hand whisker stir the liquid until the salt is dissolved.
4. Then add cream cheese and heavy cream.
5. Stir the ingredients until you get the homogenous liquid.

6. After this, add broccoli florets.
7. Preheat the air fryer to 375F.
8. Spray the air fryer basket with cooking spray from inside.
9. Pour the egg liquid in the air fryer basket.
10. Cook the omelet for 14 minutes.

Nutritional value per serving:

Calories 102, Fat 8.1, Carbs 1.5, Protein 6.2

Spiced Baked Eggs

Spiced baked eggs can be made entirely in the oven or the stove. However, bread for mopping of not optional!
Prep time and cooking time: 13 minutes | Serves: 2

Ingredients To Use:

- 2 eggs
- 1 teaspoon mascarpone
- 1/4 teaspoon ground nutmeg
- 1/4 teaspoon dried basil
- 1/4 teaspoon dried oregano
- 1/4 teaspoon dried cilantro
- 1/4 teaspoon ground turmeric
- 1/4 teaspoon onion powder
- 1/4 teaspoon salt

Step-by-Step Directions to cook it:

1. Crack the eggs in the mixing bowl and whisk them well.
2. After this, add mascarpone and stir until you get a homogenous mixture.

3. Then add all spices and mix up the liquid gently.
4. Pour it in the silicone egg molds and transfer in the air fryer basket.
5. Cook the egg cups for 3 minutes at 400F.

Calories 72, Fat 4.9, Carbs 1.1, Protein 5.9

Baked Eggs

Learning how to bake eggs in the oven is a total game changer. You can eat it on the go or at home.
Prep time and cooking time: 20 minutes | Serves: 3

- 3 eggs
- 1/2 teaspoon ground turmeric
- 1/4 teaspoon salt
- 3 bacon slices
- 1 teaspoon butter, melted

1. Brush the muffin silicone molds with 1/2 teaspoon of melted butter.
2. Then arrange the bacon in the silicone molds in the shape of circles.
3. Preheat the air fryer to 400F.
4. Cook the bacon for 7 minutes.
5. After this, brush the center of every bacon circle with remaining butter.
6. Then crack the eggs in every bacon circles, sprinkle with salt and ground turmeric.
7. Cook the bacon cups for 3 minutes more.

Calories 178, Fat 13.6, Carbs 0.9, Protein 12.6

Scotch Eggs

Cooked eggs swaddled in sausage meat, the breaded and fired. These scotch eggs are so delicious.
Prep time and cooking time: 28 minutes | Serves: 4

- 4 medium eggs, hard-boiled, peeled
- 9 oz. ground beef
- 1 teaspoon garlic powder
- 1/4 teaspoon cayenne pepper
- 1 oz. coconut flakes
- 1/4 teaspoon curry powder
- 1 egg, beaten
- 1 tablespoon almond flour
- Cooking spray

1. In the mixing bowl combine together ground beef and garlic powder.
2. Add cayenne pepper, almond flour, and curry powder.
3. Stir the meat mixture until

homogenous.
4. After this, wrap the peeled eggs in the ground beef mixture.
5. In the end, you should get meat balls.
6. Coat every ball in the beaten egg and then sprinkle with coconut flakes.
7. Preheat the air fryer to 400F.
8. Then spray the air fryer basket with cooking spray and place the meat eggs inside.
9. Cook the eggs for 13 minutes.
10. Carefully flip the scotch eggs on another side after 7 minutes of cooking.

Nutritional value per serving:

Calories 272, Fat 16, Carbs 4.3, Protein 28.6

Eggs Ramekins

A Fancy Everyday Breakfast. These eggs ramekins are so tasty and delicious and easy to make.
Prep time and cooking time: 11 minutes | Serves: 5

Ingredients To Use:

- 5 eggs
- 1 teaspoon coconut oil, melted
- 1/4 teaspoon ground black pepper

Step-by-Step Directions to cook it:

1. Brush the ramekins with coconut oil and crack the eggs inside.

2. Then sprinkle the eggs with ground black pepper and transfer in the air fryer.
3. Cook the baked eggs for 6 minutes at 355F.

Nutritional value per serving:

Calories 144, Fat 8, Carbs 9.1, Protein 8.8

Herbed Omelet

Luscious with custardy curds coddled inside a smooth, buttery skin. This herb omelet is a downright herbed egg pillow.
Prep time and cooking time: 25 minutes | Serves: 4

Ingredients To Use:

- 10 eggs, whisked
- 1/2 cup cheddar, shredded
- 2 tablespoons parsley, chopped
- 2 tablespoons chives, chopped
- 2 tablespoons basil, chopped
- Cooking spray
- Salt and black pepper to the taste

Step-by-Step Directions to cook it:

1. In a bowl, mix the eggs with all the ingredients except the cheese and the cooking spray and whisk well.
2. Preheat the air fryer at 350 degrees F, grease it with the cooking spray, and pour the eggs mixture inside.

3. Sprinkle the cheese on top and cook for 20 minutes.
4. Divide everything between plates and serve.

Nutritional value per serving:

Calories 232, Fat 12, Carbs 5, Protein 7

Olives and Eggs Mix

Olives and eggs mix are crunchy, spicy, salty and very addictive. Best serve with dressing for dipping.
Prep time and cooking time: 25 minutes | Serves: 4

Ingredients To Use:

- 2 cups black olives, pitted and chopped
- 4 eggs, whisked
- 1/4 teaspoon sweet paprika
- 1 tablespoon cilantro, chopped
- 1/2 cup cheddar, shredded
- A pinch of salt and black pepper
- Cooking spray

Step-by-Step Directions to cook it:

1. In a bowl, mix the eggs with the olives and all the ingredients except the cooking spray and stir well.
2. Heat up your air fryer at 350 degrees F, grease it with cooking spray, pour the olives and eggs mixture, spread and cook for 20 minutes.

3. Divide between plates and serve for breakfast.

Nutritional value per serving:

Calories 240, Fat 14, Carbs 5, Protein 8

Eggplant Spread

Stuffed into slits in the eggplant before its grilled. This eggplant spread is flavorful. Serve it on crispy grilled crostini.
Prep time and cooking time: 25 minutes | Serves: 4

Ingredients To Use:

- 3 eggplants
- Salt and black pepper to the taste
- 2 tablespoons chives, chopped
- 2 tablespoons olive oil
- 2 teaspoons sweet paprika

Step-by-Step Directions to cook it:

1. Put the eggplants in your air fryer's basket and cook them for 20 minutes at 380 degrees F.
2. Peel the eggplants, put them in a blender, add the rest of the ingredients, pulse well, divide into bowls and serve for breakfast.

Nutritional value per serving:

Calories 190, Fat 7, Carbs 5, Protein 3

Creamy Parmesan Eggs

Loaded with heavy cream, butter and parmesan cheese. These creamy parmesan eggs will change your mornings forever.

Prep time and cooking time: 18 minutes | Serves: 4

Ingredients To Use:

- 4 eggs
- 1 tablespoon heavy cream
- 1 oz. Parmesan, grated
- 1 teaspoon dried parsley
- 3 oz. kielbasa, chopped
- 1 teaspoon coconut oil

Step-by-Step Directions to cook it:

1. Toss the coconut oil in the air fryer basket and melt it at 385F.
2. It will take about 2-3 minutes.
3. Meanwhile, crack the eggs in the mixing bowl.
4. Add heavy cream and dried parsley.
5. Whisk the mixture.
6. Put the chopped kielbasa in the melted coconut oil and cook it for 4 minutes at 385F.
7. After this, add the whisked egg mixture, Parmesan, and stir with the help of the fork.
8. Cook the eggs for 2 minutes.
9. Then scramble them well and cook for 2 minutes more or until they get the desired texture.

Nutritional value per serving:

Calories 157, Fat 12.2, Carbs 1.5, Protein 10.7

Buttery Eggs

Life changing soft Buttery eggs. Quick and easy to make! It is best serve during breakfast.

Prep time and cooking time: 25 minutes | Serves: 4

Ingredients To Use:

- 2 tablespoons butter, melted
- 6 teaspoons basil pesto
- 1 cup mozzarella cheese, grated
- 6 eggs, whisked
- 2 tablespoons basil, chopped
- A pinch of salt and black pepper

Step-by-Step Directions to cook it:

1. In a bowl, mix all the ingredients except the butter and whisk them well.
2. Preheat your Air Fryer at 360 degrees F, drizzle the butter on the bottom, spread the eggs mix, cook for 20 minutes and serve for breakfast.

Nutritional value per serving:

Calories 207, Fat 14, Carbs 4, Protein 8

Dill Egg Rolls

One of the easiest and tastiest appetizers ever. These dill egg rolls are just plain awesome.
Prep time and cooking time: 14 minutes | Serves: 4

Ingredients To Use:

- 2 eggs, hard-boiled, peeled
- 1 tablespoon cream cheese
- 1 tablespoon fresh dill, chopped
- 1 teaspoon ground black pepper
- 4 wontons wrap
- 1 egg white, whisked
- 1 teaspoon sesame oil

Step-by-Step Directions to cook it:

1. Chop the eggs and mix them up with cream cheese, dill, and ground black pepper.
2. Then place the egg mixture on the wonton wraps and roll them into the rolls.
3. Brush every roll with whisked egg white.
4. After this, preheat the air fryer to 395F and brush the air fryer basket with sesame oil. Arrange the egg rolls in the hot air fryer and cook them for 2 minutes from each side or until the rolls are golden brown.

Nutritional value per serving:

Calories 81 Fat 4.4, Carbs 5.7, Protein 4.9

Parsley Omelet

Cheesy flavor omelet that can be serve in less than twenty minutes. Filled with fresh veggies and cheese.

Prep time and cooking time: 20 minutes | Serves: 4

Ingredients To Use:

- 4 eggs, whisked
- 1 tablespoon parsley, chopped
- 1/2 teaspoons cheddar cheese, shredded
- 1 avocado, peeled, pitted and cubed
- Cooking spray

Step-by-Step Directions to cook it:

1. In a bowl, mix all the ingredients except the cooking spray and whisk well.
2. Grease a baking pan that fits the Air Fryer with the cooking spray, pour the omelet mix, spread, introduce the pan in the machine and cook at 370 degrees F for 15 minutes.
3. Serve for breakfast.

Nutritional value per serving:

Calories 240, Fat 13, Carbs 6, Protein 9

Chapter 9: Vegetarian Recipes

Instant Air Fried Potato Chips

The beauty of air fry with the Instant Pot Duo Crisp Air Fryer Lid is that you get to fry with 70% less oil. Check out this potato chips recipe air-fried with just 1 Tablespoon of oil.

Prep time and cooking time: 60 minutes | Serves: 4

Ingredients To Use:

- 4 potatoes, slice into thin strips and soaked for 30 minutes, then drained and patted dry with a paper towel
- Salt, as desired
- 1 Tbsp. of olive oil
- 2 tsp. of chopped rosemary

Step-by-Step Directions to Cook It:

1. Mix the potato chips, salt, and oil in a bowl.
2. Transfer to the Instant Pot cooker base and cover with the Instant Pot Duo Crisp Air Fryer Lid.
3. Select the Air Fry Smart Program and set the timer to 30 minutes at 330°F
4. Divide into equal proportions, sprinkle with rosemary, and serve as a side dish

Nutritional value per serving:
Calories: 200kcal, Fat: 4g, Carbs: 14g, Protein: 5g

Delicious Air Fried Broccoli

Broccoli has a bitter taste, but when it is air-fried with the Instant Pot Duo Crisp Air Fryer Lid, it becomes better.

Prep time and cooking time: 30 minutes | Serves: 4

Ingredients To Use:

- 1 Tbsp. of duck fat
- 1 broccoli head, florets removed and set aside
- 3 garlic cloves, grated
- 1/2 lemon, juiced
- 1 Tbsp. sesame seeds

Step-by-Step Directions to Cook It:

1. Set the empty cooker base to Sauté mode and melt the duck fat.
2. Add the broccoli, lemon juice, garlic, and sesame seeds and transfer to the Instant Pot cooker base.
3. Cover with the Instant Pot Duo Crisp Air Fryer Lid and select the Air Fry Smart program.
4. Set the timer to 20 minutes at

350°F.

5. Divide into equal proportions and serve.

Calories: 132kcal, Fat: 3g, Carbs: 6g, Protein: 4g

Roasted Eggplant

The Instant Pot Duo Crisp Air Fryer Lid adds a crunchy flavor to the otherwise average vegetable.
Prep time and cooking time: 30 minutes | Serves: 6

Ingredients To Use:

- 1-1/2 pound of cubed eggplant
- 1 Tbsp. of olive oil
- 1 tsp. of garlic powder
- 1 tsp. onion powder
- 1 tsp. sumac
- 2 tsp. zaatar
- 1/2 lemon, juice
- 2 bay leaves

Step-by-Step Directions to Cook It:

1. Mix the eggplants, oil, garlic, sumac, onion, zaatar, bay leaves, and lemon juice in the inner pot of the air fryer.
2. Cover with the Instant Pot Duo Crisp Air Fryer Lid and select the Roast Smart Program.
3. Set the timer for 20 minutes at 370°F.
4. Divide into equal proportions and serve.

Nutritional value per serving:

Calories: 172kcal, Fat: 4g, Carbs: 12g, Protein: 3g

Glazed Beets

Regular beets are healthy and delicious, but when prepared with the Instant Pot Duo Crisp Air Fryer Lid, the taste is transformed, and it becomes extraordinary.
Prep time and cooking time: 50 minutes | Serves: 8

Ingredients To Use:

- 3 pounds of trimmed small beets
- 4 Tbsp. maple syrup
- 1 Tbsp. duck fat

Step-by-Step Directions to Cook It:

1. Set the empty cooker base to Sauté mode and melt the duck fat.
2. Add the maple syrup and beets to the air fryer and cover with the Instant Pot Duo Crisp Air Fryer Lid.
3. Select the Air Fry Smart Program and set the timer to 40 minutes at 350°F.
4. Divide into equal proportions and serve.

Nutritional value per serving:

Calories: 121kcal, Fat: 3g, Carbs: 3g, Protein: 4g

Vermouth Mushrooms

Air fried mushrooms can be eaten as a snack or side dish.
Prep time and cooking time: 35 minutes | Serves: 4

Ingredients To Use:

- 1 Tbsp. olive oil
- 2 pounds of white mushrooms
- 2 Tbsp. of white vermouth
- 2 tsp. of herbs de Provence
- 2 garlic cloves, grated

Step-by-Step Directions to Cook It:

1. Mix the mushrooms, oil, herbs de Provence, and garlic in a small bowl.
2. Transfer to the Instant Pot cooker base and cover with the Instant Pot Duo Crisp Air Fryer Lid.
3. Select the Air Fry Smart Program and set the timer to 20 minutes at 350°F.
4. Add the vermouth and cook for another 5 minutes.
5. Divide into equal portions and serve.

Nutritional value per serving:

Calories: 121kcal, Fat: 2g, Carbs: 7g, Protein: 4g

Roasted Peppers

Roasted bell peppers can be eaten as a side dish. The slices are crispy and crunchy. Try the recipe out now.
Prep time and cooking time: 30 minutes | Serves: 4

Ingredients To Use:

- 1 Tbsp. sweet paprika
- 1 Tbsp. olive oil
- 4 red bell peppers, chopped into strips
- 4 green bell peppers, cut into strips
- 4 yellow bell peppers, cut into strips
- 1 yellow onion, sliced
- Salt and black pepper, as desired

Step-by-Step Directions to Cook It:

1. Add the all the bell peppers to the Instant Pot cooker base.
2. Add the oil, onion, paprika, salt, and black pepper and cover with the Instant Pot Duo Crisp Air Fryer Lid.
3. Select the Roast Smart program and set the timer to 20 minutes at 350°F
4. Divide into equal proportions and serve.

Nutritional value per serving:

Calories: 142kcal, Fat: 4g, Carbs: 7g, Protein: 4g

Creamy Brussels Sprouts and Ham

The cream and spices improve the taste of the broccoli, and the ham adds flavor to the meal.
Prep time and cooking time: 35 minutes | Serves: 8

Ingredients To Use:

- 3 pounds Brussels sprouts, halved
- 1 cup of milk
- A drizzle of olive oil
- 1 pound of chopped bacon
- Salt and black pepper, as desired
- 4 Tbsp. butter
- 3 shallots, coarsely chopped
- 2 cups of heavy cream
- 1/4 tsp. of ground nutmeg
- 3 Tbsp. of prepared horseradish

Step-by-Step Directions to Cook It:

1. Preheat the Instant Pot cooker base to 370°F and add the oil, Brussels, bacon, salt, and black pepper. Toss.
2. Add the shallots, butter, heavy cream, nutmeg, horseradish, milk, and cook for another 25 minutes.
3. Divide into equal proportions and serve.

Nutritional value per serving:

Calories: 214kcal, Fat: 5g, Carbs: 12g, Protein: 5g

Garlic Potatoes

The potato is seasoned with numerous spices and cooked until it is soft enough to melt in the mouth.
Prep time and cooking time: 30 minutes | Serves: 6

Ingredients To Use:

- 2 Tbsp. of chopped parsley
- 5 garlic cloves, grated
- 1/2 tsp. of dried basil
- 1/2 tsp. of dried oregano
- 3 pounds of halved red potatoes
- 1 tsp. of dried thyme
- 2 tsp. of olive oil
- Salt and black pepper, as desired
- 2 Tbsp. of butter
- 1/3 cup of grated parmesan

Step-by-Step Directions to Cook It:

1. Mix the potato, parsley, garlic, oregano, thyme, salt, black pepper, basil, oil, and butter. Toss
2. Transfer to the Instant Pot cooker base and cover with the Instant Pot Duo Crisp Air Fryer Lid.
3. Select the Bake Smart Program and set the timer to 20 minutes at 400°F.
4. Sprinkle with the grated parmesan and divide into equal portions.
5. Serve.

Calories: 162kcal, Fat: 5g, Carbs: 7g, Protein: 5g

Crispy Ratatouille

It's packed with fresh produce, bell pepper, zucchini and yellow squash, eggplant and tomatoes. These crispy ratatouille is fun to make.

Prep time and cooking time: 14 minutes | Serves: 4

Ingredients To Use:

- Kosher salt, for salting and seasoning
- 1 small eggplant, peeled and sliced into 1/2 inch pieces
- 1 medium zucchini, sliced into 1/2 inch pieces
- 2 tbsps. olive oil
- 1 cup chopped onion
- 3 garlic cloves, minced or pressed
- 1 small green bell pepper, cut into 1/2-inch chunks (about 1 cup)
- 1 small red bell pepper, sliced into 1/2-inch chunks (about 1 cup)
- 1 rib celery, sliced (about 1 cup)
- 1 (14.5-ounce) can diced tomatoes, undrained
- 1/4 cup water
- 1/2 tsp. dried oregano
- 1/4 tsp. black pepper, ground
- 2 tbsps. fresh basil, minced
- 1/4 cup pitted green or black olives (optional)

Step-by-Step Directions to cook it:

1. Place a rack on a baking sheet. With kosher salt, very liberally salt one side of the eggplant and zucchini slices, and place them, salted-side down, on the rack. Salt the other side. Let the slices sit for 15 to 20 minutes, or until they start to exude water (you'll see it beading up on the surface of the slices and dripping into the sheet pan). Rinse the slices, and blot them dry. Cut the zucchini slices into quarters and the eggplant slices into eighths. Turn the Instant Crisp Air Fryer to "Sauté", heat the olive oil until it shimmers and flows like water. Add the onion and garlic, and sprinkle with a pinch or two of kosher salt. Cook for about 3 minutes, stirring until the onions just begin to brown. Add the eggplant, zucchini, green bell pepper, red bell pepper, celery, and tomatoes with their juice, water, and oregano.

2. Lock the pressure cooking lid on the Instant Crisp Air Fryer and then cook for 4 minutes. To get 4-minutes cook time, press "Pressure" button and use the Time Adjustment button to adjust the cook time to 4 minutes.

3. Use the quick-release method.
4. Unlock and remove the lid. Close the Air Fryer Lid, select BROIL, and set the time to 5 minutes. Select START to begin. Cook until top is browned. Stir in the pepper, basil, and olives (if using). Taste, adjust the seasoning as needed, and serve. While this vegetable dish is usually served on its own, it's great tossed with cooked pasta or served over polenta.

Calories: 149; Fat: 8g; Carbs: 20g; Protein: 4g

Avocado Fries

Avocado fries is the ultimate dish for avocado lovers. Lightly fried to crispy golden brown perfection.
Prep time and Cooking time 17 Minutes | Serves: 6

Ingredients To Use:

- 1 avocado
- 1/2 tsp. salt
- 1/2 C. panko breadcrumbs
- Bean liquid (aquafaba) from a 15-ounce can of white or garbanzo beans

Step-by-Step Directions to cook it:

1. Peel, pit, and slice up avocado.
2. Toss salt and breadcrumbs together in a bowl. Place aquafaba into another bowl.

3. Dredge slices of avocado first in aquafaba and then in panko, making sure you get an even coating.
4. Place coated avocado slices into a single layer in the Instant Crisp Air Fryer. Set temperature to 390°F, and set time to 5 minutes.
5. Serve with your favorite keto dipping sauce!

Calories: 102; Fat: 22g; Carbs: 1g, Protein:9g

Warm Quinoa And Potato Salad

Warm quinoa and potato salad is a healthy lunch, packed full of plant based protein.
Prep time and cooking time: 20 Minutes | Serves 6

Ingredients To Use:

- 1/4 cup white balsamic vinegar
- 1 tablespoon Dijon mustard
- 1 teaspoon sweet paprika
- 1/2 teaspoon ground black pepper
- 1/4 teaspoon celery seeds
- 1/4 teaspoon salt
- 1/4 cup olive oil
- 1-1/2 pounds tiny white potatoes, halved
- 1 cup blond (white) quinoa
- 1 medium shallot, minced
- 2 medium celery stalks, thinly

sliced
- 1 large dill pickle, diced

Step-by-Step Directions to cook it:

1. Whisk the vinegar, mustard, paprika, pepper, celery seeds, and salt in a large serving bowl until smooth; whisk in the olive oil in a thin, steady stream until the dressing is fairly creamy.
2. Place the potatoes and quinoa in the Instant Crisp Air Fryer ; add enough cold tap water so that the ingredients are submerged by 3 inches (some of the quinoa may float).
3. Lock the pressure cooking lid on the Instant Crisp Air Fryer and then cook for 10 minutes. To get 10-minutes cook time, press "Pressure" button and use the Time Adjustment button to adjust the cook time to 10 minutes.
4. Use the quick-release method to bring the pot's pressure back to normal.
5. Unlock and open the pot. Close the Air Fryer Lid. Select BROIL, and set the time to 5 minutes. Select START to begin. Cook until top is browned. Drain the contents of the pot into a colander lined with paper towels or into a fine-mesh sieve in the sink. Do not rinse.
6. Transfer the potatoes and quinoa to the large bowl with the dressing. Add the shallot, celery, and pickle; toss gently and set aside for a minute or two to warm up the vegetables.

Nutritional value per serving:

Calories: 244; Fat: 12g; Carbs: 2 g, Protein: 12g

Bell Pepper-Corn Wrapped in Tortilla

These bell pepper corn wrapped in tortilla are quick and easy dinner. Make ahead meals are a boon to busy homes.
Prep time and cooking time: 20 Minutes | Serves: 4

Ingredients To Use:
- 1 small red bell pepper, chopped
- 1 small yellow onion, diced
- 1 tablespoon water
- 2 cobs grilled corn kernels
- 4 large tortillas
- 4 pieces commercial vegan nuggets, chopped
- mixed greens for garnish

Step-by-Step Directions to cook it:

1. Preheat the Instant Crisp Air Fryer to 400°F.
2. In a skillet heated over medium heat, water sauté the vegan nuggets together with the onions,

bell peppers, and corn kernels. Set aside.

3. Place filling inside the corn tortillas.
4. Lock the air fryer lid. Fold the tortillas and place inside the Instant Crisp Air Fryer and cook for 15 minutes until the tortilla wraps are crispy.
5. Serve with mix greens on top.

Calories: 548; Fat: 20.7g; Carbs: 10 g, Protein: 46g

Spicy Sweet Potato Fries

Spicy sweet potato fries are the perfect vegetarian side dish. The taste is super delicious.
Prep time and cooking time: 45 Minutes | Serves: 4

Ingredients To Use:

- 2 tbsp. sweet potato fry seasoning mix
- 2 tbsp. olive oil
- 2 sweet potatoes
- Seasoning Mix:
- 2 tbsp. salt
- 1 tbsp. cayenne pepper
- 1 tbsp. dried oregano
- 1 tbsp. fennel
- 2 tbsp. coriander

Step-by-Step Directions to cook it:

1. Slice both ends off sweet potatoes and peel. Slice

lengthwise in half and again crosswise to make four pieces from each potato.
2. Slice each potato piece into 2-3 slices, then slice into fries.
3. Grind together all of seasoning mix ingredients and mix in the salt.
4. Ensure the Instant Crisp Air Fryer is preheated to 350 degrees.
5. Toss potato pieces in olive oil, sprinkling with seasoning mix and tossing well to coat thoroughly.
6. Add fries to Instant Crisp Air Fryer basket. Lock the lid of the air fryer. Set temperature to 350°F, and set time to 27 minutes. Select START to begin.
7. Remove the basket and thoroughly stir the fries. Switch off the Instant Crisp Air Fryer and allow to cook for about 12 minutes until the fries are golden.

Nutritional value per serving:

Calories: 89; Fat: 14g; Carbs: 3 g, Protein: 8g

Creamy Spinach Quiche

It is a classic recipe you will wnjoy. It is best serve after lunch.
Prep time and cooking time: 30 Minutes | Serves: 4

Ingredients To Use:

- Premade quiche crust, chilled and rolled flat to a 7-inch round

- eggs
- 1/4 cup of milk
- Pinch of salt and pepper
- 1 clove of garlic, peeled and finely minced
- 1/2 cup of cooked spinach, drained and coarsely chopped
- 1/4 cup of shredded mozzarella cheese
- 1/4 cup of shredded cheddar cheese

Step-by-Step Directions to cook it:

1. Preheat the Instant Crisp Air Fryer to 360 degrees.
2. Press the premade crust into a 7-inch pie tin, or any appropriately sized glass or ceramic heat-safe dish. Press and trim at the edges if necessary. With a fork, pierce several holes in the dough to allow air circulation and prevent cracking of the crust while cooking.
3. In a mixing bowl, beat the eggs until fluffy and until the yolks and white are evenly combined.
4. Add milk, garlic, spinach, salt and pepper, and half the cheddar and mozzarella cheese to the eggs. Set the rest of the cheese aside for now, and stir the mixture until completely blended. Make sure the spinach is not clumped together, but rather spread among the other ingredients.

5. Pour the mixture into the pie crust, slowly and carefully to avoid splashing. The mixture should almost fill the crust, but not completely – leaving a ¼ inch of crust at the edges.
6. Lock the air fryer lid. Set the air-fryer timer for 15 minutes. After15 minutes, the Instant Crisp Air Fryer will shut off, and the quiche will already be firm and the crust beginning to brown. Sprinkle the rest of the cheddar and mozzarella cheese on top of the quiche filling. Reset the Instant Crisp Air Fryer at 360 degrees for 5 minutes. After 5 minutes, when the Instant Crisp Air Fryer shuts off, the cheese will have formed an exquisite crust on top and the quiche will be golden brown and perfect. Remove from the Instant Crisp Air Fryer using oven mitts or tongs, and set on a heat-safe surface to cool for a few minutes before cutting.

Nutritional value per serving:

Calories: 89; Fat: 14g; Carbs: 3 g, Protein: 8g

Cauliflower Rice

Cauliflower rice is so healthy and easy to do. You don't have to go a restaurant just to eat this.
Prep time and cooking time: 25 Minutes | Serves: 4

Ingredients To Use:

- tsp. turmeric
- 1 C. diced carrot
- 1/2 C. diced onion
- 2 tbsp. low-sodium soy sauce
- 1/2 block of extra firm tofu
- 1/2 C. frozen peas
- 2 minced garlic cloves
- 1/2 C. chopped broccoli
- 1 tbsp. minced ginger
- 1 tbsp. rice vinegar
- 1-1/2 tsp. toasted sesame oil
- 2 tbsp. reduced-sodium soy sauce
- 3 C. riced cauliflower

Step-by-Step Directions to cook it:

1. Crumble tofu in a large bowl and toss with all the Round one ingredient.
2. Lock the air fryer lid. Preheat the Instant Crisp Air Fryer to 370 degrees, set temperature to 370°F, and set time to 10 minutes and cook 10 minutes, making sure to shake once.
3. In another bowl, toss ingredients from Round 2 together.
4. Add Round 2 mixture to Instant Crisp Air Fryer and cook another 10 minutes, ensuring to shake 5 minutes in.
5. Enjoy!

Nutritional value per serving:

Calories: 67; Fat: 8g; Carbs: 0g,

Protein: 3g

Buttery Carrots With Pancetta

Delicious Buttery Carrots with Pancetta is good and tasty. Your family will love this recipe.
Prep time and cooking time: 17 Minutes | Serves 4 - 6

Ingredients To Use:

- 4 ounces pancetta, diced
- 1 medium leek, white and pale green parts only, sliced lengthwise, washed, and thinly sliced
- 1/4 cup moderately sweet white wine, such as a dry Riesling
- 1 pound baby carrots
- 1/2 teaspoon ground black pepper
- 2 tablespoons unsalted butter, cut into small bits

Step-by-Step Directions to cook it:

1. Put the pancetta in the Instant Crisp Air Fryer turned to the "Air Fry" function and use the Time Adjustment button to adjust the cook time to 5 minutes. Add the leek; cook, often stirring, until softened. Pour in the wine and scrape up any browned bits at the bottom of the pot as it comes to a simmer.
2. Add the carrots and pepper; stir

well. Scrape and pour the contents of the Instant Crisp Air Fryer into a 1-quart, round, high-sided soufflé or baking dish. Dot with the bits of butter. Lay a piece of parchment paper on top of the dish, then a piece of aluminum foil. Seal the foil tightly over the baking dish.

3. Set the Instant Crisp Air Fryer rack inside, and pour in 2 cups water. Use aluminum foil to build a sling for the baking dish; lower the baking dish into the cooker.

4. Lock the Pressure cooking lid on the Instant Crisp Air Fryer and then cook for 7 minutes. To get 7-minutes cook time, press "Pressure" button and use the Time Adjustment button to adjust the cook time to 7 minutes.

5. Use the quick-release method to return the pot's pressure to normal.

6. Close the Air Fryer Lid. Select BROIL, and set the time to 5 minutes. Select START to begin. Cook until top is browned.

7. Unlock and open the pot. Use the foil sling to lift the baking dish out of the cooker. Uncover, stir well, and serve.

Nutritional value per serving:

Calories: 67; Fat: 8g; Carbs: 0g, Protein: 3g

Chapter 10: Snacks and Desserts

Sweet Potato Cheesecake

If you think strawberry cheesecake is the best, then you haven't tried this lovely potato cheesecake cooked with the Instant Pot Duo Crisp Air Fryer Lid.

Prep time and cooking time: 15 minutes | Serves: 4

Ingredients To Use:

- 4 Tbsp. of melted butter
- 6 ounces of soft mascarpone
- 8 ounces of soft cream cheese
- 2/3 cup of crumbled graham crackers
- 3/4 cup of milk
- 1 tsp. vanilla extract
- 2/3 cup of sweet potato puree
- 1/4 tsp. cinnamon powder

Step-by-Step Directions to Cook It:

1. Mix the butter and crackers in a small bowl. Press the mixture to the bottom of a cake pan that fits the Instant Pot cooker base. Refrigerate for a few minutes.
2. In a separate bowl, mix the cheese, potato puree, cinnamon, milk, vanilla, and mascarpone. Whisk until well-combined.
3. Spread the cinnamon mixture on the crust and transfer to the

Instant Pot cooker base. Cover with the Instant Pot Duo Crisp Air Fryer Lid and select the Bake Smart Program.
4. Set the timer to 4 minutes at 300°F.
5. Keep in the refrigerator for a few minutes before serving.

Nutritional value per serving:

Calories: 172kcal, Fat: 4g, Carbs: 8g, Protein: 3g

Cashew Bars

The bars are delicious and yummy. Try this recipe out now with the Instant Pot Duo Crisp Air Fryer Lid

Prep time and cooking time: 25 minutes | Serves: 6

Ingredients To Use:

- 1/3 cup of honey
- 1/4 cup of almond meal
- 1 Tbsp. almond butter
- 1-1/2 cup of cashews, chopped
- 4 dates, chopped
- 3/4 cup of coconut, shredded
- 1 Tbsp. chia seeds

Step-by-Step Directions to Cook It:

1. Mix the almond meal, almond butter, and honey in a bowl.
2. Add the coconut, cashews, dates,

and chia seeds.

3. Spread the almond mix on a lined baking sheet that is appropriate for the Instant Pot cooker base and cover with the Instant Pot Duo Crisp Air Fryer Lid. Press well.
4. Set the timer for 15 minutes at 300°F.
5. Allow to cool, cut into medium bars, and serve.

Nutritional value per serving:

Calories: 121kcal, Fat: 4g, Carbs: 5g, Protein: 6g

Mandarin Pudding

This is a lovely delicacy that is common in South Asia. Let the pudding speak to your taste buds.
Prep time and cooking time: 1 hour | Serves: 8

Ingredients To Use:

- 1 mandarin, peeled and sliced
- 2 mandarins, juiced
- 2 Tbsp. of brown sugar
- 4 ounces of soft butter
- 2 eggs, beaten
- 3/4 cup of sugar
- 3/4 cup white flour
- 3/4 cup of ground almonds
- Honey, for garnish

Step-by-Step Directions to Cook It:

1. Lightly grease an oven-safe loaf pan with some soft butter and sprinkle with brown sugar.
2. Arrange the mandarin slices on the pan.
3. Mix the rest of the butter with the eggs, sugar, almonds, mandarin juice, and flour. Pour this over the mandarin slices in the pan.
4. Cover with the Instant Pot Duo Crisp Air Fryer Lid and select the Bake smart Program. Set the timer to 40 minutes at 360°F.
5. Transfer to a plate and drizzle with honey. Serve.

Nutritional value per serving:

Calories: 200kcal, Fat: 5g, Carbs: 8g, Protein: 6g

Sweet Squares

If you have a sweet tooth, then this recipe is perfect for you. It has all the right ingredients in an excellent combination.
Prep time and cooking time: 40 minutes | Serves: 6

Ingredients To Use:

- 1 cup of flour
- 1/2 cup of soft butter
- 1 cup of sugar
- 1/4 cup of powdered sugar
- 2 tsp. lemon peel, grated
- 2 Tbsp. lemon juice
- 2 eggs, whisked
- 1/2 tsp. baking powder

1. Mix the flour, sugar, and butter in a medium bowl.
2. Press the mixture to the bottom of a springform pan that fits the Instant Pot cooker base.
3. Cover with the Instant Pot Duo Crisp Air Fryer Lid and select the Bake Smart Program.
4. Set the timer to 14 minutes at 350°F.
5. In a separate bowl, mix the sugar, lemon juice and peel, eggs, and baking powder with an electric mixer. Spread this mix over the crust in the pan.
6. Cover with the Instant Pot Duo Crisp Air Fryer Lid and bake for another 15 minutes.
7. Allow to cool, then cut into squares and serve.

Nutritional value per serving:

Calories: 100kcal, Fat: 4g, Carbs: 12g, Protein: 1g

Figs and Coconut Butter Mix

Coconut makes everything better. This coconut and fig recipe is a delicacy fit for kings. Serve as a dessert after the main meal.
Prep time and cooking time: 10 minutes | Serves: 3

Ingredients To Use:

- 2 Tbsp. coconut butter
- 12 figs, halved
- 1/4 cup of sugar
- 1 cup of toasted almonds, chopped

Step-by-Step Directions to Cook It:

1. Set the empty cooker base to Sauté mode and melt the butter.
2. Add the almonds, figs, and sugar to the inner pot, then cover with the Instant Pot Duo Crisp Air Fryer Lid.
3. Select the Bake Smart program and set the timer for 4 minutes at 300°F.
4. Divide into equal portions and serve.

Nutritional value per serving:

Calories: 170kcal, Fat: 4g, Carbs: 7g, Protein: 9g

Passion Fruit Pudding

Passion fruit has a tangy tropical taste that reminds you of the beach. This pudding is well-flavored and delicious.
Prep time and cooking time: 50 minutes | Serves: 6

Ingredients To Use:

- 1 cup of Paleo passion fruit curd
- 4 passion fruits, pulp and seeds
- 3 and 1/2 ounces maple syrup

- 3 medium eggs, whisked
- 2 ounces of melted ghee
- 3-1/2 ounces of almond milk
- 1/2 cup of almond flour
- 1/2 tsp. baking powder

Step-by-Step Directions to Cook It:

1. Mix half of the fruit curd with the passion fruit pulp and seeds. Scoop the thoroughly combined mixture into 6 oven-safe ramekins.
2. Mix the whisked eggs, ghee, maple syrup, leftover curd, baking powder, flour, and milk in a bowl. Thoroughly combine and scoop into the ramekins.
3. Introduce the ramekins to the Instant Pot cooker base and cover with the Instant Pot Duo Crisp Air Fryer Lid.
4. Select the Bake Smart program and set the timer for 40 minutes at 200°F.
5. Allow pudding to cool and serve.

Nutritional value per serving:

Calories: 430kcal, Fat: 22g, Carbs: 7g, Protein: 8g

Chocolate and Pomegranate Bars

Chocolate is always a treat for everyone, and when you combine it with pomegranate bars, it becomes exquisite.

Prep time and cooking time: 2 hours 10 minutes | Serves: 6

Ingredients To Use:

- 1/2 cup of milk
- 1 tsp. vanilla extract
- 1-1/2 cup of dark chocolate, chopped
- 1/2 cup of chopped almonds
- 1/2 cup of pomegranate seeds

Step-by-Step Directions to Cook It:

1. In a medium pan placed over low heat, boil the milk and chocolate for 5 minutes.
2. Remove from heat and add the vanilla, 1/2 of the pomegranate seeds, and 1/2 of the almond nuts.
3. Pour the mixture into a lined baking pan and sprinkle with salt and the leftover pomegranate and almonds.
4. Cover with the Instant Pot Duo Crisp Air Fryer Lid and select the Bake Smart program.
5. Set the timer to 4 minutes at 300°F.
6. Remove and keep in the refrigerator for 2 hours.
7. Serve.

Nutritional value per serving:

Calories: 68kcal, Fat: 1g, Carbs: 6g, Protein: 1g

Blueberry Pudding

An excellent blueberry pudding recipe contains all the ingredients in the right proportion. This recipe is one of those great recipes.
Prep time and cooking time: 35 minutes | Serves: 6

Ingredients To Use:

- 2 cups of flour
- 2 cups of rolled oats
- 8 cups of blueberries
- 1 stick butter, melted
- 1 cup of chopped walnuts
- 3 Tbsp. maple syrup
- 2 Tbsp. of chopped rosemary

Step-by-Step Directions to Cook It:

1. Grease a baking pan and add the blueberries. Set aside.
2. Add the rolled oats, flour, walnuts, butter, rosemary, and maple syrup to the blueberries.
3. Transfer to the Instant Pot cooker base and cover with the Instant Pot Duo Crisp Air Fryer Lid.
4. Select the Bake Smart program and set the timer for 25 minutes at 350°F.
5. Allow to cool, then serve.

Nutritional value per serving:

Calories: 150kcal, Fat: 3g, Carbs: 7g, Protein: 4g

Paneer Cheese Balls

Made from spices, onions, processed cheese and paneer. These paneer cheese balls is so delicious.
Prep Time and cooking time: 25 minutes | Serving: 6

Ingredients To Use:

- 1 cup paneer, crumbled
- 1 cup cheese, grated
- 1 potato, boiled and mashed
- 1 onion, chopped finely
- 1 green chili, chopped finely
- 1 teaspoon red chili flakes
- salt to taste
- 4 tbsp. coriander leaves, chopped finely
- 1/2 cup all-purpose flour
- 3/4 cup of water
- Breadcrumbs as needed

Step-by-Step Directions to cook it:

1. Mix flour with water in a bowl and spread the breadcrumbs in a tray.
2. Add the rest of the Ingredients: to make the paneer mixture.
3. Make golf ball-sized balls out of this mixture.
4. Dip each ball in the flour liquid then coat with the breadcrumbs.
5. Place the cheese balls in the Instant Pot Duo and spray it with cooking spray.
6. Put on the Air Fryer lid and seal it.
7. Hit the "Air fry Button" and select 15 minutes of cooking time, then

press "Start."
8. Once the Instant Pot Duo beeps, remove its lid.
9. Serve.

Nutritional value per serving:

Calories: 227; Fat: 10g; Carbs: 3 g, Protein: 10g

Russet Potato Hay

With only one tablespoon of oil to makes this crispy and golden brown. Russet potato hay is good for snacks.
Prep Time and cooking time: 25 minutes | Serving: 4

Ingredients To Use:

- 2 russet potatoes
- 1 tablespoon olive oil
- Salt and black pepper to taste

Step-by-Step Directions to cook it:

1. Pass the potatoes through a spiralizer to get potato spirals.
2. Soak these potato spirals in a bowl filled with water for about 20 minutes.
3. Drain and rinse the soaked potatoes then pat them dry.
4. Toss the potato spirals with salt, black pepper, and oil in a bowl.
5. Spread the seasoned potato spirals in the Air Fryer Basket.
6. Set this Air Fryer Basket in the Instant Pot duo.
7. Put on the Air Fryer lid and seal it.
8. Hit the "Air fry Button" and select

15 minutes of cooking time, then press "Start."
9. Toss the potato spiral when halfway cooked then resume cooking.
10. Once the Instant Pot Duo beeps, remove its lid.
11. Serve.

Nutritional value per serving:

Calories: 104; Fat: 4 g; Carbs: 1 g, Protein: 2 g

Onion Rings

These onion rings are crispy and delicious. Easy to prepare and easy to cook. It is best serve during snacks.
Prep Time and cooking time: 20 minutes | Serving: 4

Ingredients To Use:

- 3/4 cup flour
- 1 large yellow onion, sliced and rings separated
- 1/4 tsp. garlic powder
- 1/4 tsp. paprika
- 1 cup almond milk
- 1 large egg
- 1/2 cup cornstarch
- 1-1/2 teaspoons of baking powder
- 1 teaspoon salt
- 1 cup bread crumbs
- cooking spray

Step-by-Step Directions to cook it:

1. Whisk flour with baking powder,

salt, and cornstarch in a bowl.

2. Coat the onion rings with this dry flour mixture and keep them aside.
3. Beat egg with milk in a bowl and dip the rings in this mixture.
4. Place the coated rings in the Air Fryer Basket and set it inside the Instant Pot Duo.
5. Spray the onion rings with cooking oil. Put on the Air Fryer lid and seal it.
6. Hit the "Air fry Button" and select 10 minutes of cooking time, then press "Start."
7. Flip the rings when cooked halfway through.
8. Once the Instant Pot Duo beeps, remove its lid.
9. Serve.

Nutritional value per serving:

Calories: 319; Fat: 4 g; Carbs: 6 g, Protein: 10 g

Breaded Avocado Fries

Breaded avocado fries is easy to make. With just five ingredients and magical addictive properties.
Prep Time and cooking time: 17 minutes | Serving: 4

Ingredients To Use:

- 1/4 cup all-purpose flour
- 1/2 teaspoon ground black pepper
- 1/4 teaspoon salt
- 1 egg
- 1 teaspoon water
- 1 ripe avocado, peeled, pitted and sliced
- 1/2 cup panko bread crumbs
- cooking spray

Step-by-Step Directions to cook it:

1. Whisk flour with salt and black pepper in one bowl.
2. Beat egg with water in another and spread the crumbs in a shallow tray.
3. First coat the avocado slices with the flour mixture then dip them into the egg.
4. Drop off the excess and coat the avocado with panko crumbs liberally.
5. Place all the coated slices in the Air Fryer Basket and spray them with cooking oil.
6. Set the Air Fryer Basket inside the Instant Pot Duo.
7. Put on the Air Fryer lid and seal it.
8. Hit the "Air fry Button" and select 7 minutes of cooking time, then press "Start."
9. Flip the fries after 4 minutes of cooking and resume cooking.
10. Once the Instant Pot Duo beeps, remove its lid.
11. Serve fresh.

Nutritional value per serving:

Calories: 201; Fat: 12 g; Carbs: 1 g, Protein: 5 g

Buffalo Chicken Strips

Buffalo chicken strips made with a classic buttermilk soaked extra crispy chicken. It is best serve during dinner.

Prep Time and cooking time: 18 minutes | Serving: 4

Ingredients To Use:

- 1/2 cup Greek yogurt
- 1/4 cup egg
- 1-1/2 tablespoon hot sauce
- 1 cup panko bread crumbs
- 1 tablespoon sweet paprika
- 1 tablespoon garlic pepper seasoning
- 1 tablespoon cayenne pepper
- 1-pound chicken breasts, cut into strips

Step-by-Step Directions to cook it:

1. Mix Greek yogurt with hot sauce and egg in a bowl.
2. Whisk bread crumbs with garlic powder, cayenne pepper, and paprika in another bowl.
3. First, dip the chicken strips in the yogurt sauce then coat them with the crumb's mixture.
4. Place the coated strips in the Air Fryer Basket and spray them with cooking oil.
5. Set the Air Fryer Basket inside the Instant Pot Duo.
6. Put on the Air Fryer lid and seal it.
7. Hit the "Air fry Button" and select 16 minutes of cooking time, then press "Start."
8. Flip the chicken strips after 8 minutes of cooking then resume Air fearing.
9. Once the Instant Pot Duo beeps, remove its lid.
10. Serve.

Nutritional value per serving:

Calories: 368; Fat: 11 g; Carbs: 3 g, Protein: 40 g

Sweet Potato Chips

Sweet potato chips are best serve during snacks. Easy, crispy and perfect with just a sprinkle of salt.

Prep Time and cooking time: 23 minutes | Serving: 2

Ingredients To Use:

- 1 teaspoon avocado oil
- 1 medium sweet potato, peeled and sliced
- 1/2 teaspoon Creole seasoning

Step-by-Step Directions to cook it:

1. Toss the sweet potato with avocado oil and creole seasoning in a bowl.
2. Spread the potato slices in the Air Fryer Basket and spray them with oil.
3. Set the Air Fryer Basket in the Instant Pot Duo.
4. Put on the Air Fryer lid and seal it.

5. Hit the "Air fry Button" and select 13 minutes of cooking time, then press "Start."
6. Toss the potato slices after 7 minutes of cooking and resume air frying.
7. Once the Instant Pot Duo beeps, remove its lid.
8. Serve fresh.

Nutritional value per serving:

Calories: 55; Fat: 0 g; Carbs: 3 g, Protein: 1 g

Corn Nuts

Thanks to the air fryer, this corn nuts is so crunch, salty and addictive. Feel free to add additional flavors such as taco seasoning, chili powder, BBQ seasoning, Ranch powder and cajun seasoning.

Prep Time and cooking time: 30 minutes | Serving: 6

Ingredients To Use:

- 14 oz. giant white corn
- 3 tablespoons vegetable oil
- 1-1/2 teaspoons salt

Step-by-Step Directions to cook it:

1. Soak white corn in a bowl filled with water and leave it for 8 hours.
2. Drain the soaked corns and spread them in the Air Fryer Basket.

3. Leave to dry for 20 minutes after patting them dry with a paper towel.
4. Add oil and salt on top of the corns and toss them well.
5. Set the Air Fryer Basket in the Instant Pot.
6. Put on the Air Fryer lid and seal it.
7. Hit the "Air fry Button" and select 20 minutes of cooking time, then press "Start."
8. Shake the corns after every 5 minutes of cooking, then resume the function.
9. Once the Instant Pot Duo beeps, remove its lid.
10. Serve.

Nutritional value per serving:

Calories: 128; Fat: 7 g; Carbs: 2 g, Protein: 2 g

Tempura Vegetables

Tempura vegetables is so delicious and crispy. Just try to not absorb oil when deep fried.

Prep Time and cooking time: 20 minutes | Serving: 4

Ingredients To Use:

- 1/2 cup all-purpose flour
- 1/2 teaspoon salt, divided, or more to taste
- 1/2 teaspoon ground black pepper
- 2 eggs
- 2 tablespoons water

- 1 cup panko bread crumbs
- 2 teaspoons vegetable oil
- 1/2 cup whole green beans
- 1/2 cup asparagus spears
- 1/2 cup red onion rings
- 1/2 cup sweet pepper rings
- 1/2 cup avocado wedges
- 1/2 cup zucchini slices

Step-by-Step Directions to cook it:

1. Whisk flour with black pepper and salt in a shallow dish.
2. Beat eggs with water in a bowl and mix panko with oil in another tray.
3. Coat all the veggies with flour mixture first, then dip them in egg and finally in the panko mixture to a coat.
4. Shake off the excess and keep the coated veggies in separate plates.
5. Set half of the coated vegetables in a single layer in the Air Fryer Basket.
6. Place the basket in the Instant Pot Duo and spray them with cooking oil.
7. Put on the Air Fryer lid and seal it.
8. Hit the "Air fry Button" and select 10 minutes of cooking time, then press "Start."
9. Once the Instant Pot Duo beeps, remove its lid.
10. Transfer the fried veggies to the serving plates and cooking the

remaining half using the same steps.
11. Serve.

Nutritional value per serving:

Calories: 275; Fat: 9 g; Carbs: 4 g, Protein: 9 g

Shrimp a La Bang Sauce

Crispy sweet and spicy shrimp. These shrimp a la bang sauce is perfect on a family gathering.
Prep Time and cooking time: 22 minutes | Serving: 6

Ingredients To Use:

- 1/2 cup mayonnaise
- 1/4 cup sweet chili sauce
- 1 tablespoon sriracha sauce
- 1/4 cup all-purpose flour
- 1 cup panko bread crumbs
- 1-pound raw shrimp, peeled and deveined
- 1 head loose-leaf lettuce
- 2 green onions, chopped, or to taste

Step-by-Step Directions to cook it:

1. Whisk mayonnaise with sriracha, chili sauce in a bowl until smooth.
2. Spread flour in one plate and panko in the other.
3. Place flour on a plate. Place panko on a separate plate.
4. First coat the shrimp with the flour, then dip in mayonnaise

mixture and finally coat with the panko.

5. Arrange the shrimp in the Air Fryer Basket in a single layer. (do not overcrowd)
6. Set the Air Fryer Basket in the Instant Pot Duo.
7. Put on the Air Fryer lid and seal it.
8. Hit the "Air fry Button" and select 12 minutes of cooking time, then press "Start."
9. Once the Instant Pot Duo beeps, remove its lid.
10. Air fry the remaining shrimp in the same way.
11. Garnish with lettuce and green onion.
12. Serve.

Nutritional value per serving:

Calories: 285; Fat: 9 g; Carbs: 7 g, Protein: 20 g

Chapter 11: Yogurt and Cake

Tomato Cake

Tomato can also be used as the main ingredient of a cake recipe. Try this recipe out now, and you won't be disappointed.

Prep time and cooking time: 40 minutes | Serves: 4

Ingredients To Use:

- 1-1/2 cups of flour
- 1 tsp. of cinnamon powder
- 1 tsp. of baking powder
- 1 tsp. of baking soda
- 3/4 cup of maple syrup
- 1 cup tomatoes chopped
- 1/2 cup of olive oil
- 2 Tbsp. apple cider vinegar

Step-by-Step Directions to Cook It:

1. Mix the flour, baking powder, cinnamon, baking soda, and maple syrup. Stir.
2. In a separate bowl, mix the olive oil, vinegar, and tomatoes.
3. Combine the two mixtures in a bowl and add to a greased springform pan that fits the Instant Pot cooker base.
4. Cover with the Instant Pot Duo Crisp Air Fryer Lid. Select the Bake Smart Program.
5. Set the timer for 30 minutes for 360°F.
6. Allow the cake to cool and serve.

Nutritional value per serving:

Calories: 153kcal, Fat: 2g, Carbs: 25g, Protein: 4g

Tangerine Cake

Spice up your cake with this citrus fruit, and your life will never remain the same.

Prep time and cooking time: 30 minutes | Serves: 8

Ingredients To Use:

- 3/4 cup of sugar
- 2 cups flour
- 1/4 cup olive oil
- 1/2 cup milk
- 1 tsp. cider vinegar
- 1/2 tsp. vanilla extract
- 2 lemons, juiced and zested
- 1 tangerine, juiced and zested
- Tangerine segments, for garnish

Step-by-Step Directions to Cook It:

1. Mix the flour and sugar in a bowl.
2. In a separate bowl, mix the milk, oil, vanilla, vinegar, tangerine juice and zest, lemon juice, and zest. Stir until well-combined.
3. Add the flour to the mixture, then transfer to an oven-safe baking

dish.

4. Place in the Instant Pot cooker base and cover with the Instant Pot Duo Crisp Air Fryer Lid.
5. Select the Bake Smart Program and set the timer for 20 minutes at 360°F.
6. Serve.

Calories: 190kcal, Fat: 1g, Carbs: 4g, Protein: 4g

Cauliflower Cakes

This recipe produces a soft and fluffy cauliflower rice cake. Try it now to enjoy the delicious goodness.
Prep time and cooking time: 20 minutes | Serves: 6

Ingredients To Use:

- 3-1/2 cups of cauliflower rice
- 2 medium eggs
- 1/4 cup of white flour
- 1/2 cup of grated parmesan
- Salt and black pepper, as desired
- Cooking spray

Step-by-Step Directions to Cook It:

1. Season the cauliflower rice with salt and black pepper and remove the excess water.
2. Transfer the rice to another bowl, add the flour, eggs, salt, black pepper, and parmesan. Stir well.
3. Shape the cakes and transfer to the grease Instant Pot cooker

base. Cover with the Instant Pot Duo Crisp Air Fryer Lid.

4. Select the Bake Smart Program and set the timer to 10 minutes at 400°F. Turn halfway.
5. Serve as a side dish.

Calories: 125kcal, Fat: 2g, Carbs: 8g, Protein: 3g

Ricotta and Lemon Cake

Lemon adds a sharp, pleasant aftertaste to this recipe. Try it out now to discover its magic.
Prep time and cooking time: 1 hour 20 minutes | Serves: 4

Ingredients To Use:

- 8 eggs, beaten
- 3 pounds of ricotta cheese
- 1/2 pound of sugar
- 1 lemon, grated and zested
- 1 orange, grated and zested
- Butter

Step-by-Step Directions to Cook It:

1. Mix the eggs, sugar, lemon, orange zest, and cheese in a small bowl. Stir until well-combined.
2. Grease a springform baking pan with the butter and spread the ricotta mix in it.
3. Transfer to the Instant Pot cooker base and cover with the Instant Pot Duo Crisp Air Fryer

Lid.
4. Select the Bake Smart Program and set the timer for 30 minutes at 390°F
5. Allow the cake to cool before serving.

Calories: 110kcal, Fat: 3g, Carbs: 3g, Protein: 4g

Maple Cupcakes

The maple syrup adds a distinctive taste to the apple cake. Every bite of this maple cake recipe comes with a burst of flavor.
Prep time and cooking time: 30 minutes | Serves: 4

Ingredients To Use:

- 4 Tbsp. of butter
- 4 eggs, beaten
- 1/2 cup of pure applesauce
- 2 tsp. of cinnamon powder
- 1 tsp. vanilla extract
- 1/2 apple, cored and chopped
- 4 tsp. of maple syrup
- 3/4 cup of white flour
- 1/2 tsp. of baking powder

Step-by-Step Directions to Cook It:

1. Set the empty cooker base to Sauté mode and melt the butter. Add the applesauce, vanilla, maple syrup, and eggs. Fry for a few minutes, then set aside.
2. Mix the flour, baking powder,

cinnamon, and apples in a bowl, then scoop into a cupcake pan.
3. Transfer to the Instant Pot cooker base and cover with the Instant Pot Duo Crisp Air Fryer Lid.
4. Select the Bake Smart Recipes and set the timer to 20 minutes and 350°F.
5. Allow the cupcake to cool and transfer to a platter and serve.

Calories: 150kcal, Fat: 3g, Carbs: 5g, Protein: 4g

Lime Cheesecake

Lime may be sour but, in this recipe, it brings out the flavor of the coconut cream cheese.
Prep time and cooking time: 4 hours 10 minutes | Serves: 10

Ingredients To Use:

- 2 Tbsp. of melted butter
- 2 tsp. of sugar
- 4 ounces of flour
- 1/4 cup of shredded coconut

Filling Ingredients

- 1 pound of cream cheese
- 1 lime, grated and zested
- 1 lime, juiced
- 2 cups of hot water
- 2 sachets of lime jelly

Step-by-Step Directions to Cook It:

1. Mix the coconut, flour, sugar, and butter in a small bowl. Pour the mixture to the bottom a baking pan and press well.
2. Melt the jelly sachets with hot water until it completely dissolves.
3. Add the cream cheese, dissolved jelly, lime juice, and zest to a bowl and stir well.
4. Pour the cream cheese mix over the crust in the baking pan and transfer to the Instant pot cooker base.
5. Cover with the Instant Pot Duo Crisp Air Fryer Lid and select the Bake Smart program. Set the timer for 4 minutes at 300°F.
6. Allow to cool then serve.

Nutritional value per serving:

Calories: 260kcal, Fat: 23g, Carbs: 5g, Protein: 7g

Instant pot yogurt

I love yogurt, o you love yogurt? The good news is that you don't have to buy store-bought yogurt anymore. With your instant pot, you can make as much yogurt as possible.
Prep Time and Cooking Time: 9 hours 5 minutes| Serves: 16

Ingredients to use:

- 1/2 gallon milk
- 2 tbsp. yogurt with cultures

Step-by-step Directions to Cook It:

1. Pour milk in the instant pot then press the yogurt function until the display reads boil.
2. Once the IP beeps, the boiling time has elapsed. Remove the lid and test if the temperature is 180F. Let the inner pot of the instant pot rest in the instant pot for 5 minutes.
3. Let the milk cool to 115 F.
4. Skim off the yogurt skin then whisk it in the milk.
5. Place the inner pot in the instant pot, secure the lid, and select the yogurt button.
6. Once the instant pot beeps, the yogurt is ready. Pour in a jar or in a glass and store in the fridge

Nutritional value per serving:

Calories: 89kcal, Carbs: 5g Fat: 2g, Protein: 3g

Instant pot Greek Yogurt

This creamy and thick Greek yogurt is very simple to make at home in your instant pot. You just need two ingredients to bring it together.
Prep Time and Cooking Time: 25 minutes| Serves: 2

Ingredients to use:

- 1 gallon Whole Milk
- 2 tbsp. yogurt Starter

Step-by-step Directions to Cook It:

1. Pour milk in the instant pot then press the yogurt function until the display reads boil.
2. Once the IP beeps, the boiling time has elapsed. Remove the lid and test if the temperature is 180F. Let the inner pot of the instant pot rest in the instant pot for 5 minutes.
3. Let the milk cool to 115 F.
4. Skim off the yogurt skin then whisk it in the milk.
5. Place the inner pot in the instant pot, secure the lid, and select the yogurt button.
6. Once the instant pot beeps, the yogurt is ready. Pour in a jar or in a glass and store in the fridge.
7. Use yogurt strainer to strain the yogurt in the fridge or 2 hours. The whey should be translucent or clear. If the whey is cloudy add another cheesecloth layer.
8. Serve your Greek yogurt and enjoy it.

Nutritional value per serving:

Calories: 118kcal, Carbs: 6g Fat: 1g, Protein: 20g

White Chocolate Berry Cheesecake

What could be better? White chocolate, cheesecake and blueberry topping! It is best serve during desserts.
Prep time and cooking time: 15 minutes | Serves: 4

Ingredients To Use:

- 8 oz. cream cheese, softened
- 2 oz. heavy cream
- 1/2 tsp. Splenda
- 1 tsp. raspberries
- 1 tbsp. Da Vinci Sugar-Free syrup, white chocolate flavor

Step-by-Step Directions to cook it:

1. Whip together the ingredients to a thick consistency.
2. Divide in cups.
3. Refrigerate.
4. Serve!

Nutritional value per serving:

Calories 243; Fat 0 g; Carbs 0 g; Protein 0 g

Chocolate Cheesecake

Rich, moist, dense and hugely chocolate. This recipe is everything you want it to be.
Prep time and cooking time: 60 minutes | Serves: 4

- 4 oz. cream cheese
- 1/2 oz. heavy cream
- 1 tsp. Sugar Glycerite
- 1 tsp. Splenda
- 1 oz. Enjoy Life mini chocolate chips

Step-by-Step Directions to cook it:

1. Combine all the ingredients except the chocolate to a thick consistency.
2. Fold in the chocolate chips.
3. Refrigerate in serving cups.
4. Serve!

Nutritional value per serving:

Calories 330; Fat 19 g; Carbs 34 g; Protein 6 g

Berry Layer Cake

Decorated with swirls and rosettes of frosting flavored. These berry layer cake is sweet and moist inside your mouth.
Prep time and cooking time: 8 minutes | Serves: 1

Ingredients To Use:

- 1/4 lemon pound cake
- 1/4 cup whipping cream
- 1/2 tsp. Truvia
- 1/8 tsp. orange flavor
- 1 cup of mixed berries

Step-by-Step Directions to cook it:

1. Using a sharp knife, divide the lemon cake into small cubes.
2. Dice the strawberries.
3. Combine the whipping cream, Truvia, and orange flavor.
4. Layer the fruit, cake and cream in a glass.
5. Serve!

Nutritional value per serving:

Calories 350; Fat 19 g; Carbs 40 g; Protein 8 g

Banana Chocolate Cake

Mixed with seasonings, these banana chocolate cake makes a delightful way to enjoy a classic flavor combination.
Prep time and cooking time: 30 minutes | Serves: 10

Ingredients To Use:

- 1 stick softened butter
- 1/2 cup sugar
- 1 egg
- 1 bananas, mashed
- 2 tbsp. maple syrup
- 2 cups flour
- 1/4 tsp. anise star, ground
- 1/4 tsp. ground mace
- 1/4 tsp. ground cinnamon
- 1/4 tsp. crystallized ginger
- 1/2 tsp. vanilla paste
- Pinch of kosher salt
- 1/2 cup cocoa powder

1. Beat together the softened butter and sugar to combine well.
2. Mix together the egg, mashed banana and maple syrup using a whisk.
3. Combine the two mixtures, stirring well until pale and creamy.
4. Add in the flour, anise star, mace, cinnamon, crystallized ginger, vanilla paste, salt, and cocoa powder. Mix well to form the batter.
5. Grease two cake pans with cooking spray.
6. Transfer the batter into the cake pans and place them in the Air Fryer.
7. Cook at 330°F for 30 minutes. Frost with chocolate glaze if desired

Nutritional value per serving:

Calories 260; Fat 11 g; Carbs 37 g; Protein 3 g

Lemon Butter Pound Cake

This lemon butter pound cake is for lemon lovers. Drizzled with a tart lemon glaze and flavored with lemon zest and juice.

Prep time and cooking time: 20 minutes | Serves: 8

Ingredients To Use:

- 1 stick softened butter
- 1 cup sugar
- 1 medium egg
- 1-1/4 cups flour
- 1 tsp. butter flavoring
- 1 tsp. vanilla essence
- Pinch of salt
- 3/4 cup milk
- Grated zest of 1 medium-sized lemon
- For the Glaze:
- 2 tbsp. freshly squeezed lemon juice

Step-by-Step Directions to cook it:

1. In a large bowl, use a creamer to mix together the butter and sugar. Fold in the egg and continue to stir.
2. Add in the flour, butter flavoring, vanilla essence, and salt, combining everything well.
3. Pour in the milk, followed by the lemon zest, and continue to mix.
4. Lightly brush the inside of a cake pan with the melted butter.
5. Pour the cake batter into the cake pan.
6. Place the pan in the Air Fryer and bake at 350°F for 15 minutes.
7. After removing it from the fryer, run a knife around the edges of the cake to loosen it from the pan and transfer it to a serving plate.

8. Leave it to cool completely.
9. In the meantime, make the glaze by combining with the lemon juice.
10. Pour the glaze over the cake and let it sit for a further 2 hours before serving.

Nutritional value per serving:

Calories 200; Fat 10 g; Carbs 29 g; Protein 2 g

Swirled German Cake

Starts with a cake mix and a cheesecake filling. These swirled german cake is the most amazing homemade frosting!
Prep time and cooking time: 25 minutes | Serves: 8

Ingredients To Use:

- 1 cup flour
- 1 tsp. baking powder
- 1 cup sugar
- 1/8 tsp. kosher salt
- 1/4 tsp. ground cinnamon
- 1/4 tsp. grated nutmeg
- 1 tsp. orange zest
- 1 stick butter, melted
- 2 eggs
- 1 tsp. pure vanilla extract
- 1/4 cup milk
- 2 tbsp. unsweetened cocoa powder

Step-by-Step Directions to cook it:

1. Take a round pan that is small enough to fit inside your Air Fryer and lightly grease the inside with oil.
2. In a bowl, use an electric mixer to combine the flour, baking powder, sugar, salt, cinnamon, nutmeg, and orange zest.
3. Fold in the butter, eggs, vanilla, and milk, incorporating everything well.
4. Spoon a quarter-cup of the batter to the baking pan.
5. Stir the cocoa powder into the rest of the batter.
6. Use a spoon to drop small amounts of the brown batter into the white batter. Swirl them together with a knife.
7. Place the pan in the Air Fryer and cook at 360°F for about 15 minutes.
8. Remove the pan from the fryer and leave to cool for roughly 10 minutes.

Nutritional value per serving:

Calories 251; Fat 21 g; Carbs 13 g; Protein 5 g

Double Chocolate Cake

Double chocolate cake is easy to make. Mixed with seasonings and let the air fryer do the magic!
Prep time and cooking time: 45 minutes | Serves: 8

Ingredients To Use:

- 1/2 cup sugar
- 1-/4 cups flour
- 1 tsp. baking powder
- 1/3cup cocoa powder
- 1/4 tsp. ground cloves
- 1/8 tsp. freshly grated nutmeg
- Pinch of table salt
- 1 egg
- 1/4 cup soda of your choice
- 1/4 cup milk
- 1/2 stick butter, melted
- 2 oz. bittersweet chocolate, melted
- 1/2 cup hot water

Step-by-Step Directions to cook it:

1. In a bowl, thoroughly combine the dry ingredients.
2. In another bowl, mix together the egg, soda, milk, butter, and chocolate.
3. Combine the two mixtures. Add in the water and stir well.
4. Take a cake pan that is small enough to fit inside your Air Fryer and transfer the mixture to the pan.
5. Place a sheet of foil on top and bake at 320°F for 35 minutes.
6. Take off the foil and bake for further 10 minutes.
7. Frost the cake with buttercream if desired before serving.

Nutritional value per serving:

Calories 241353; Fat 4 g; Carbs 21 g; Protein 3 g

Chapter 12: Slow Cooking Recipes

Seafood Chowder

This special chowder dish is great for the holidays when everyone is too busy to monitor the food. Try it out on hectic days.

Prep time and cooking time: 5 hours | Serves: 8

Ingredients To Use:

- 1 can of cream of potato soup
- 1 can of cream of mushroom soup
- 2-1/2 cup of milk
- 4 medium carrots, chopped
- 1 large onion, chopped
- 2 potatoes, cubed
- 2 celery stalks, chopped
- 1 can of chopped clams, drained
- 1 can of medium shrimp, drained
- 4 ounces of flaked crabmeat
- 5 cooked and crumbled bacon strips

Step-by-Step Directions to Cook It:

1. Add the potato soup, milk, and mushroom soup to the Instant Pot cooker base.
2. Stir in the potatoes, carrots, celery, and onions.
3. Cover with the Dehydration tray and Instant Pot Duo Crisp Air Fryer Lid
4. Select the Dehydrate Smart Program and set the timer to 4 hours.
5. After 4 hours, add the shrimp, clams, and crab. Replace the cover and set the timer for 20 minutes.
6. Serve into plates and garnish with bacon.

Nutritional value per serving:

Calories: 124kcal, Fat: 12g, Carbs: 15g, Protein: 9g

Potatoes and Tomatoes Mix

The Instant Pot Duo Crisp Air Fryer Lid cooks this meal exquisitely. The potato is soft and just melts in the mouth.

Prep time and cooking time: 3 hours 10 minutes | Serves: 4

Ingredients To Use:

- 1-1/2 pounds of red potatoes, cut into quarters
- 2 Tbsp. olive oil
- 1 pint of cherry tomatoes
- 1 tsp. sweet paprika
- 1 Tbsp. of chopped rosemary
- Salt and black pepper, as desired
- 3 garlic cloves, grated

1. Mix the potatoes, tomatoes, paprika, oil, garlic, rosemary, pepper, and salt in a bowl.
2. Transfer the mixture to the Instant Pot cooker base and cover with the broil/dehydration tray and Instant Pot Duo Crisp Air Fryer Lid.
3. Select the Dehydrate Smart program and set the timer for 16 minutes at 300°F for 3 hours.
4. Divide into equal portions and serve.

Nutritional value per serving:

Calories: 192kcal, Fat: 4g, Carbs: 30g, Protein: 3g

Slow-Cooked Duck Breasts

The slow cooking will allow the optimal absorption of the spices by the duck. The taste of the meat product with this recipe is out of this world.
Prep time and cooking time: 3 hours | Serves: 2

Ingredients To Use:

- 2 duck breasts
- 1 cup of white wine
- 1/4 cup of soy sauce
- 2 garlic cloves, minced
- 6 tarragon sprigs
- Salt and black pepper, as desired
- 1 tablespoon butter

- 1/4 cup sherry wine

Step-by-Step Directions to Cook It:

1. Mix the duck breasts with the wine, soy, tarragon, garlic, pepper, and salt in a bowl.
2. Transfer the contents of the bowl to the Instant Pot cooker base.
3. Cover with the dehydration tray and Instant Pot Duo Crisp Air Fryer Lid.
4. Select the Dehydrate Smart Program and set the timer for 3 hours.
5. Discard the soup and serve the duck into plates.

Nutritional value per serving:

Calories: 475kcal, Fat: 12g, Carbs: 10g, Protein: 48g

Chinese Duck Legs

The time required for cooking this recipe is worth it because the taste of the is exquisite.
Prep time and cooking time: 3 hours 20 minutes | Serves: 2

Ingredients To Use:

- 2 duck legs
- 2 dried chilies, finely chopped
- 1 Tbsp. olive oil
- 2-star anises
- 1 bunch spring onions, chopped
- 4 ginger slices
- 1 Tbsp. oyster sauce
- 1 Tbsp. of soy sauce

- 1 tsp. sesame oil
- 14 ounces of water
- 1 Tbsp. of rice wine

1. Set the empty cooker base to Sauté mode and heat the oil. Stir in the chili, star anise, sesame oil, rice wine, oyster sauce, water, and soy sauce—Brown for 6 minutes.
2. Add the spring onions and duck legs. Cover with the dehydration tray and Instant Pot Duo Crisp Air Fryer Lid.
3. Select the Dehydrate Smart program and set the timer for 3 hours at 320°F.
4. Divide into equal portions and serve.

Nutritional value per serving:

Calories: 300kcal, Fat: 12g, Carbs: 10g, Protein: 48g

Balsamic Beef

The 4 hours spent cooking allows the beef to absorb the sauce and vinegar. It results in a fantastic meal.

Prep time and cooking time: 4 hours 10 minutes | Serves: 6

Ingredients To Use:

- 1 beef roast
- 1 Tbsp. Worcestershire sauce
- 1/2 cup of balsamic vinegar
- 1 cup of beef stock
- 1 Tbsp. honey
- 1 Tbsp. of soy sauce
- 4 garlic cloves, grated

Step-by-Step Directions to Cook It:

1. In an oven-safe baking dish, add the roast, Worcestershire sauce, vinegar, honey, soy sauce, and garlic.
2. Transfer the dish to the Instant Pot cooker base and cover with the dehydration tray and Instant Pot Duo Crisp Air Fryer Lid.
3. Select the Dehydrate Smart Program and set the timer for 4 hours at 300°F
4. Divide into equal portions and serve.

Nutritional value per serving:

Calories: 311kcal, Fat: 7g, Carbs: 20g, Protein: 16g

Chapter 13: Sauté Recipes

New England Haddock Chowder

Haddock's firm meat has a delicate flavor, and this makes it ideal for a fish chowder recipe.

Prep time and cooking time: 30 minutes | Serves: 10

Ingredients To Use:

- 1/2 cup of butter
- 3 medium onions, chopped
- 5 medium potatoes, cubed
- 4 tsp. salt
- 1/2 tsp. of black pepper
- 2 pounds of haddock fillets, divided into portions
- 1 quart of scalded milk
- 12 ounces of evaporated milk

Step-by-Step Directions to Cook It:

1. Set the empty cooker base to Sauté mode and melt 1/4 of the butter. Stir in the onions and brown for about 2 minutes.
2. Add the potatoes, pepper, salt, and 3 cups of boiling water. To with the haddock fillets and cover with the Instant Pot Duo Crisp Air Fryer Lid.
3. Select the Broil Smart Program and set the timer to 25 minutes at 350°F.
4. Remove the cover and stir in the evaporated milk, scalded milk, and leftover butter.
5. Season with salt and pepper if desired.
6. Serve.

Nutritional value per serving:

Calories: 173kcal, Fat: 13g, Carbs: 10g, Protein: 9g

Halibut Chowder

The fish used in this recipe can be substituted with salmon or tuna, but the tender chunks of halibut does the magic perfectly.

Prep time and cooking time: 15 minutes | Serves: 8-10

Ingredients To Use:

- 2 Tbsp. butter
- 8 scallions, chopped
- 2 garlic cloves, grated
- 4 cans of cream of potato soup
- 2 cans of cream of mushroom soup
- 4 cups of milk
- 8 ounces of cream cheese, cubed
- 1-1/2 pounds of halibut fillets, cubed
- 1-1/2 cup of frozen sliced carrots
- 1-1/2 cup of frozen corn

- 1/4 tsp. of cayenne pepper

Step-by-Step Directions to Cook It:

1. Set the empty cooker base to Sauté mode and melt the butter. Stir in the scallions and garlic. Fry for about 2 minutes.
2. Add the potato soup, milk, mushroom soup, and cream cheese.
3. Add the carrots, corn, and fish, then cover with the Instant Pot Duo Crisp Air Fryer Lid and select the Broil Smart Program.
4. Set the timer for 10 minutes at 350°F.
5. Divide into equal portions and serve. Sprinkle with cayenne pepper if desired

Nutritional value per serving:

Calories: 133kcal, Fat: 10g, Carbs: 14g, Protein: 6g

Filet Mignon and Mushroom Sauce

A classic recipe that can be made right in your home with the Instant Pot Duo Crisp Air Fryer Lid.
Prep time and cooking time: 35 minutes | Serves: 4

Ingredients To Use:

- 12 mushrooms, sliced
- 1 shallot, chopped
- 4 fillet mignons

- 2 garlic cloves, minced
- 2 Tbsp. olive oil
- 1/4 cup of Dijon mustard
- 1/4 cup of wine
- 1-1/4 cup of coconut cream
- 2 Tbsp. of chopped parsley
- Salt and black pepper, as desired

Step-by-Step Directions to Cook It:

1. Set the empty cooker base to Sauté mode and heat the oil. Stir in the scallions and garlic—Fry for about 3 minutes.
2. Add the mushrooms and cook for another 4 minutes.
3. Add the wine and boil until it evaporates.
4. Add the mustard, coconut cream, salt, black pepper, and parsley.
5. Cover with the Instant Pot Duo Crisp Air Fryer Lid and select the Broil smart Program. Set the timer to 10 minutes at 360°F.
6. Divide into equal portions and serve. Garnish with the mushroom sauce.

Nutritional value per serving:

Calories: 340kcal, Fat: 12g, Carbs: 14g, Protein: 23g

Simple Braised Pork

The steps to make the recipe may be simple, but the taste is definitely not. Try out this recipe to experience a remarkable combination of flavors.

Prep time and cooking time: 80 minutes | Serves: 4

- 2 pounds of pork loin roast, deboned and cubed
- 4 Tbsp. of melted butter
- Salt and black pepper, as desired
- 2 cup of chicken stock
- 1/2 cup of dry white wine
- 2 garlic cloves, grated
- 1 tsp. of chopped thyme
- 1 thyme spring
- 1 bay leaf
- 1/2 yellow onion, chopped
- 2 Tbsp. white flour
- 1/2 pound of red grapes

Step-by-Step Directions to Cook It:

1. Season the pork with salt and black pepper, coat with 2 tablespoons of the melted butter, then transfer to the Instant Pot cooker base.
2. Cover with the Instant Pot Duo Crisp Air Fryer Lid and select the Roast Smart Program. Set the timer to 8 minutes at 370°F.
3. When ready, transfer the contents to a bowl.
4. Set the now empty cooker base to Sauté mode and melt the leftover butter. Stir in the onions and garlic. Fry for about 2 minutes.
5. Add the wine, salt, black pepper, stock, flour, thyme, bay leaf, and stir.
6. Add the roasted pork cubes and toss until well-combined. Then cover with Instant Pot Duo Crisp Air Fryer Lid.
7. Set the timer for 30 minutes at 360°F.
8. Divide into equal portions and serve.

Nutritional value per serving:

Calories: 320kcal, Fat: 4g, Carbs: 29g, Protein: 38g

Instant Air-Fried Japanese Duck Breasts

The duck breasts are air-fried to perfection with Instant Pot Duo Crisp Air Fryer Lid.
Prep time and cooking time: 30 minutes | Serves: 6

Ingredients To Use:

- 6 boneless duck breasts
- 4 Tbsp. of soy sauce
- 1-1/2 tsp. five-spice powder
- 2 Tbsp. of honey
- Salt and black pepper, as desired
- 20 ounces of chicken stock
- 4 ginger slices
- 4 Tbsp. of hoisin sauce
- 1 tsp. of sesame oil

Step-by-Step Directions to Cook It:

1. Mix the five-spice, soy sauce,

black pepper, salt, and honey in a small bowl.

2. Coat the duck breast with the soy mixture and set aside.
3. Set the empty cooker base to Sauté mode and heat the hoisin sauce, sesame oil, and ginger. Cook for 3 minutes. Set aside.
4. Transfer the duck to the now-empty Instant Pot cooker base and cover with the Instant Pot Duo Crisp Air Fryer Lid.
5. Select the Air Fry Smart Program and set the timer for 15 minutes at 400°F.
6. Serve the duck into plates and drizzle with the prepared hoisin sauce.

Nutritional value per serving:

Calories: 336kcal, Fat: 12g, Carbs: 25g, Protein: 33g

CONCLUSION

If you want it all, a combination of versatility and effectiveness in your kitchen then this Instant Pot Duo Crisp Air Fryer Lid is a gadget you must acquire. The instant pot significantly shortens the cooking time of foods while the air fryer adds amazing crispness to food that no one can resist. Not forgetting, it a two in one appliance so saves on space if you are short of counter space.

APPENDIX I: Cooking Timetable

DAY	BREAKFAST	SNACK	LUNCH	DINNER
1	Mushroom Congee	Garlic and Parmesan Green Beans Fries	Spare Ribs	Italian Chicken Thighs
2	Tomato Pepper Frittata	Instant pot Chicken Taco Soup	salt and pepper shrimp	BBQ Ribs
3	Green Rice Porridge	Bacon Egg Muffins	Instant pot hamburger soup	T Bone steak
4	Baked Eggs	Turkey Patties	Stuffed Peppers	Instant Pot Air fryer Lid Salmon
5	Breakfast Porridge	Easy green beans	Creamy Chicken Thighs	Pork Chops
6	Veggie Omelet	Easy Crisp Chicken Wings	BBQ Bacon Meatloaf	Instant Pot Beef Stew
7	Mushroom Congee	Sweet Potato Bites	Salmon with Dill Sauce	Crisp Pork Ribs
8	Egg Soufflé	Tomato Egg Muffins	Countryside Ribs	Instant pot Air fryer Lid Cod
9	Instant pot Congee	Crispy Falafel	Instant pot Chicken Taco Soup	Easy Instant pot with Air fryer lid Ribs
10	Baked Eggs	Chicken Fritters	Fish Sticks	Beef Taquitos
11	Butternut squash Rice Porridge	Popcorn Shrimp	Honey Garlic Ribs	Lemon Pepper Chicken

12	Veggie Omelet	Healthy Kale Muffins	Baked Cod Fillet	BBQ Bacon Meatloaf
13	Instant pot porridge	Greek Egg Muffins	Breaded Turkey Breast	Crumbled Fish
14	Tomato Mushroom Frittata	Chicken Skewers	Frozen Meatballs	Frozen Meatballs

APPENDIX II: Conversion Table

	Default Temp	Temp Range	Suggested use	Default Cooking time	Cooking time Range
Air Fry	400°F	180°F - 400°F 82°C - 204°C	Fries, chicken wings, shrimp	00:18	00:01-01:00
Roast	380°F	180°F - 400°F 82°C - 204°C	Beef, lamb, pork, poultry, vegetables, scalloped potatoes etc.	00:40	00:01-01:00
Bake	365°F	180°F - 400°F 82°C - 204°C	Light fluffy cakes, buns, pastries	00:30	00:01-01:00
Broil	400°F	Not adjustable	Melt cheese on nachos or French onion	00:08	00:01-01:00
Dehyd rate	125°F	105°F - 165°F	Fruit leather, dried veggies, jerky etc.	07:00	01:00-72:00